HIKE
POINT REYES

D0888785

Hike. Contemplate what makes you happy and what makes you happier still. Follow a trail or blaze a new one. **Hike**. Think about what you can do to expand your life and someone else's. **Hike**. Slow down. Gear up. **Hike**. Connect with friends. Re-connect with nature.

Hike. Shed stress. Feel blessed. **Hike** to remember. **Hike** to forget. **Hike** for recovery. **Hike** for discovery. **Hike**. Enjoy the beauty of providence. **Hike**. Share the way, The Hiker's Way, on the long and winding trail we call life.

HIKE
POINT REYES

BY

JOHN MCKINNEY

TheTrailmaster.com

HIKE Point Reyes By John McKinney

ISBN: 978-0-934161-82-4
Book Design by Lisa DeSpain
Cartography by Tom Harrison (TomHarrisonMaps.com)
HIKE Series Editor: Cheri Rae

PHOTOS: David Abercombie, p. 105; courtesy California Coastal Commission, p. 127; courtesy Marin County Parks p. 137; courtesy National Park Service, pp. 18, 33, 38, 49, 62, 97, 112, 132; Frank Schulenburg, pp. 83, 86, 88, 114. Map p. 116 courtesy of National Park Service.

Published by Olympus Press and The Trailmaster, Inc. TheTrailmaster.com (Visit our site for a complete listing of all Trailmaster publications, products, and services.)

CONTENTS

VI For the Birds

Take it from someone who's walked the whole California coast: the trails in Point Reyes National Seashore are among the very best to be found along the entire 1,600-mile California Coastal Trail.

HIKE ON.

Point Reyes literally and figuratively sticks out and stands out from California's straight-trending coast north of San Francisco

EVERY TRAIL TELLS A STORY.

INTRODUCTION
HIKE POINT REYES

With forested ridges, wild and open coastal bluffs, and deserted beaches, Point Reyes National Seashore is an unforgettable place to ramble.

I've liked hiking Point Reyes ever since I discovered it back during my college days, but I really grew extra fond of it when I led week-long hiking adventures around the peninsula during the first decade of the 21st century. Sometimes when you have the experience of leading others along favorite trails, you learn to admire a place all the more.

I usually had about a dozen hikers with me, walkers from across the nation as well as from Europe, clients of an upscale British walking vacation company. We walked the Rift Zone Trail to the back door of Point Reyes Seashore Lodge, our "base camp," then set out on each day to discover more of the many wonders of the peninsula: Bear Valley, Arch Rock, Mt. Wittenberg, Abbotts Lagoon, Chimney

Rock, Point Reyes Lighthouse, Heart's Desire Beach, Tomales Bay and Tomales Point.

I delight in the whole Point Reyes experience: kayaking Tomales Bay, cycling the back roads, camping, cheese-tasting, wildflower walks and lighthouse tours. I've hiked Point Reyes with friends, family and schoolchildren and everyone who ventures into this area seems to experience—and retain—some of the peninsula's magic.

In hindsight, conservationists believe that the drawn-out preservation process (a 30-year struggle) benefited Point Reyes because in the interim attitudes shifted from parks-as-playgrounds to parks-as-nature preserves.

So few roads or recreation facilities were constructed here, and I say thank God for that. The area's three tiny towns—Olema, Point Reyes Station, Inverness—have remained very small. San Franciscans have an altogether different attitude toward their wilderness-next-door than, say, Bostonians have toward summer-crowded Cape Cod National Seashore.

Bear Valley is the busy hub of Point Reyes National Seashore, and there's not a hotel or restaurant in sight. Lots of trails to hike, though: 40 miles of trail thread through the valley, and to the ridges and beaches beyond.

More than a hundred miles of trail meandering through the national seashore beckon the hiker to explore wide grasslands, Bishop pine and Douglas fir forest, chaparral-cloaked coastal ridges and windswept beaches. The paths range from easy beach walks and nature hikes to rugged mountain rambles. If you want to plan a backpacking trip, Point Reyes has four hike-in camps available by reservation.

And take it from someone who has walked the entire length of the California coast: the coastal trails in Point Reyes National Seashore are among the finest along the entire 1,600-mile California Coastal Trail.

Hike smart, reconnect with nature and have a wonderful time on the trail.

Hike on.

—John McKinney

Author John McKinney: "I love hiking Point Reyes. You will, too."

POINT REYES
NATIONAL SEASHORE

Geography

Bounded on three sides by more than 50 miles of bay and ocean frontage, the point of Point Reyes, described as hammer-headed—or wing-shaped—literally and figuratively sticks out and stands out from California's fairly straight-trending coast north of San Francisco.

Point Reyes is a great place to conduct a time-motion study of the San Andreas Fault. Evidence of both slow- and fast-moving forces can be found at the national seashore. In fact, the peninsula is geologically separated from nearly all the rest of the continental U.S. by that fault zone.

Hike along the earthquake rift zone, tramp along creeks flowing through the peninsula's fissures, and look down from the ridges at Olema Valley, the 1906 quake's epicenter.

You'll see wave-torn rocks on the craggy coast that match rocks in the Tehachapi Mountains more than 300 miles to the south. And many plants and shrubs found on the west side of the fault are pre-Ice Age relics not found on the east side.

Natural Attractions

Point Reyes is a haven for birds; the seashore makes *Audubon* magazine's "Top Ten National Seashores" list. A diversity of habitats—seashore, forest, chaparral, and more—is one reason the bird count exceeds 430 species. Because Point Reyes thrusts 10 miles into the Pacific, it lures many winter migrants. Limantour and Drake *esteros* (estuaries) are resting and feeding areas for many species of shorebirds and waterfowl.

Other wildlife-watching opportunities abound. Hikers frequently spot black-tailed deer and a resident tule elk herd roams the Tomales Point area. The populations of non-native axis and fallow deer and the recommendation for their removal from the national seashore has generated much local controversy.

Migrating California gray whales travel by close to the Point Reyes Lighthouse. Elephant seals have colonized the shores near Chimney Rock and harbor seals and sea lions haul-out on the peninsula's isolated beaches.

Point Reyes also features Douglas fir forests and slopes dotted with Bishop pine. Spring wildflower displays are spectacular.

History

When British explorer Sir Francis Drake arrived on these shores in 1579, he must have felt right at home, considering Point Reyes' resemblance to Britain's shores. Long before—and after—European discovery, the native Coast Miwok lived well off the land's bounty: elk, deer, fish, shellfish, acorns, berries and much more.

Since the 1850s, cows have grazed the lush grasses of the peninsula, and such dairy operations continue today. Butter produced here was particularly prized by San Francisco gourmands.

As early as the 1930s, the National Park Service worked to purchase Point Reyes and add it to the park system. The price tag for Depression-mired America was too steep at that time, and then World War II halted all park plans.

During the post-war housing boom of the 1950s, real estate developers sought to carve up the peninsula into golf courses, residential and commercial parcels. The park service, Marin conservationists, and concerned Californians rallied to the peninsula's protection. In 1962, President John F. Kennedy signed into law the bill establishing Point Reyes National Seashore.

Parts of the Seashore are still commercially farmed though NPS all visitor impacts. Some 30 thousand acres of the national seashore's wildest terrain is designated as wilderness.

Administration

The National Park Service is the steward of the 71, 028-acre national seashore. Because parts of the peninsula are commercially farmed, it has national seashore rather than national park status. NPS manages environmental impacts and visitor services for the peninsula, most of Tomales Bay and portions of the Golden Gate National Recreation Area, such as Olema Valley, that border the national seashore.

The National Park Service manages the national seashore to protect wildlife, and sometimes closes certain hiking trails and areas. For example in 2019, when storms and high tides brought 200 elephant seals ashore, park authorities closed entry to Drakes Beach because it was unsafe for visitors to walk from the parking lot to the beach.

More examples: Parts of Point Reyes Beach are closed from March 1 to September 30 to protect snowy plover nests and chicks. From March 1 through June 30, the park closes Drakes Estero and the western end of Limantour Spit to protect harbor seals during pupping season.

Lands adjacent to the national seashore including Tomales Bay State Park and Marconi Conference Center. Point Reyes Bird Observatory and Audubon Canyon Ranch.

Contact: Point Reyes National Seashore, 1 Bear Valley Road, Point Reyes Station, CA 94956. Call 415-464-5100, visit nps.gov/pore. The park's stellar nonprofit support organization is Point Reyes National Seashore Association (ptreyes.org).

*Alamere Falls is that rare California waterfall
that cascades to the beach.*

EVERY TRAIL TELLS A STORY.

I

Palomarin & Five Brooks

HIKE ON.

PALOMARIN &
ALAMERE FALLS

Palomarin & Alamere Falls

Coast Trail

From Palomarin to Alamere Falls is 8.2 miles round trip with 300-foot elevation gain

Along with its United Kingdom-like moors, weirs, glens and vales, Point Reyes has its "Lake District." Five lakes—Bass, Pelican, Crystal, Ocean and Wildcat—were created in part by movement along the nearby San Andreas Fault.

Coast Trail zigzags and roller-coasters along, serves up ocean vistas and leads to Alamere Falls that cascades in spectacular fashion 50 feet over the coastal cliffs to the beach below.

DIRECTIONS: From Stinson Beach, drive 4.5 miles north and take the turnoff (Olema-Bolinas Road) to Bolinas. At Mesa Road, turn right and travel 4.5 miles to trailhead parking at road's end.

THE HIKE: Climb a staircase and join Coast Trail, an old farm road that turns north and ascends into a stand of eucalyptus. After 0.1 mile, Coast Trail junctions a west-branching side trail leading to Palomarin Beach and contours onto the cliff edge. Coast Trail is bordered by coyote bush and black sage, and, in springtime, brightened by foxgloves, lupine, morning glory, cow parsnip and paintbrush.

After a mile of tracing the edge of the bluffs, the trail turns inland, descends into a gully and climbs again back to the blufftops. Coast Trail soon repeats this maneuver.

About 2.25 miles from the trailhead, intersect Lake Ranch Trail leading, among other places, to Five Brooks Trailhead off Highway 1. Hike another 0.7 mile past a couple of ponds to Bass Lake, a tranquil spot shaded by Douglas fir. Another 0.25 mile and the route junctions a closed (recently removed) path to Crystal Lake.

Continue on Coast Trail, which descends from the woods to scrub community, serves up views of triangular-shaped Pelican Lake, and reaches an unsigned junction about 3.5 miles from the trailhead.

A 0.4 mile-long side trail leads coastward to overlook Double Point, two shale outcroppings enclosing a bay where seals haul-out on a small beach. Offshore stand Stormy Stacks.

Beyond this junction is another signed for Alamere Falls. The path parallels willow-lined

Alamere Creek north (right) of the trail. Descend to the eroded bluffs near the top of the falls.

Many hikers are content to safely contemplate the falls from a rocky platform adjacent to the cascade and watch it tumble to the beach. If you insist on a bottom-up view of the falls, cross Alamere Creek (do not attempt this at times of high water), and carefully pick your way down the cliffs to the beach. Either way you look at it, Alamere Creek comes to a spectacular end in the form of the falls cascading over the coastal bluffs.

Double-back to Coast Trail. Return the same way or consider adding about 2.5 more miles to the journey by heading north. After crossing Alamere Creek, the trail forks: Wildcat Trail and Coast Trail lead to Wildcat Camp and beach access. The two trails skirt Ocean Lake and Wildcat Lake, and form a handy loop.

Coast Trail leads to Pelican Lake and other small lakes in the park's "Lake District"

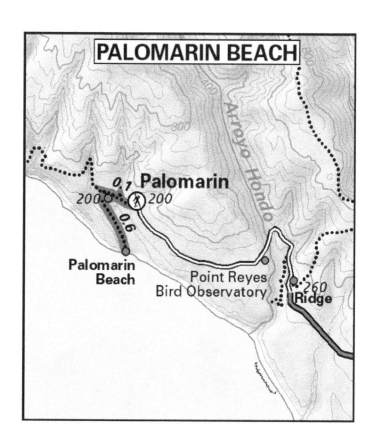

PALOMARIN BEACH

Palomarin

Palomarin Beach

Point Reyes Bird Observatory

Ridge

Palomarin Beach

Palomarin Beach Trail

1. 4 miles round trip with 250-foot elevation gain

Located on the far south end of the National Seashore, Palomarin Beach offers a brief intro to famed Coast Trail and fine tide pools. To fully appreciate Palomarin's intertidal zone, hike the beach at low tide.

DIRECTIONS: From Stinson Beach, drive 4.5 miles north and take the turnoff (Olema-Bolinas Road) to Bolinas. At Mesa Road, turn right and travel 4.5 miles to the large trailhead parking area at road's end.

THE HIKE: Follow Coastal Trail amidst eucalyptus groves 0.1 mile to an unsigned trail located at a National Park Service map/information display. Join Palomarin Beach Trail as it steeply descends eroded slopes to the beach. Tide pools are just down-coast.

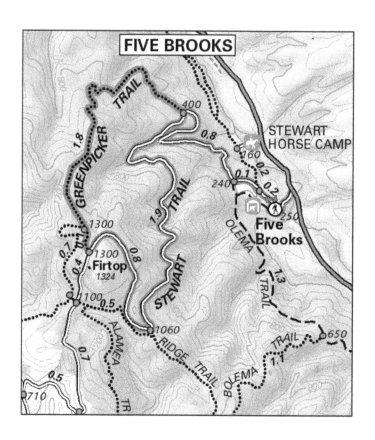

FIVE BROOKS & FIRTOP

STEWART, GREENPICKER TRAILS

7.4 miles round trip with 1,000-foot elevation gain

Five Brooks is one of those downright weird landscapes rearranged by action along the very, very nearby San Andreas Fault. Two of the five brooks—Olema Creek and Pine Gulch Creek—are parallel watercourses, hardly a quarter-mile apart, and yet they flow in opposite directions!

The favorite hiker's loop from Five Brooks is actually one of the few national seashore trails where the ocean is not an overwhelming presence; in fact, it's a no-show on this trail where trees predominate. And thank goodness for the tall trees. The 1995 Vision Fire ravaged the national seashore's conifer population, but the trees around Five Brooks escaped the conflagration.

Stewart and Greenpicker trails explore fittingly named Firtop, a fir-surrounded meadow rated "PG"—Picnicking Great. The summit of Firtop

(1,324 feet), the national seashore's second highest peak, offers a fine lunch stop but no panoramic views. In previous lives, Stewart Trail served as a logging road and U.S. Army road, and is now a wide hiking trail, occasionally used by NPS maintenance crews to service Wildcat Camp.

DIRECTIONS: From Highway 1, some 9 miles north of Stinson Beach and 3.5 miles south of Olema, turn west at the signed turnoff for Five Brooks and drive 0.25 mile to the large parking area.

THE HIKE: Begin at the gated dirt road that soon leads past a shallow pond. After a few minutes of walking, encounter the Douglas fir that will accompany you for much of the journey. Continue on your wooded way on the wide path to junction Olema Valley Trail at 0.4 mile.

Continue north with Stewart Trail as the wide road begins to climb. (It's a moderate ascent, but a relentless one, that continues all the way to the top of Firtop.) The trail bends and switchbacks, heading west to intersect Greenpicker Trail at the 1.1-mile mark.

Join Greenpicker Trail, a footpath, for a more aggressive ascent into the fir forest. The path switchbacks amidst sword ferns and huckleberry patches. Peer through the trees for vistas of slices of Bolinas Ridge and Olema Valley.

Heading toward the summit ridge the new and improved Greenpicker Trail (NPS completed a re-route a few years ago) continue to a meadow atop Firtop's summit and an intersection with Stewart Trail at the 3.0-mile mark.

After your time atop Firtop, join Stewart Trail, which begins with a brief climb east before dropping through the forest onto the east face of Inverness Ridge. The moderate descent on the dirt road (fragments of asphalt remain from the days when it was a paved route) bears south to a junction with Ridge Trail at 3.8 miles.

Continue on Stewart Trail past towering firs. Near the end of its descent, the route turns west into ravine, then swings east and finally north to junction Stewart Trail at 6.1 miles.

Now rejoin Stewart Trail, retracing your steps on a 1.3-mile descent southeast back to the Five Brooks Trailhead.

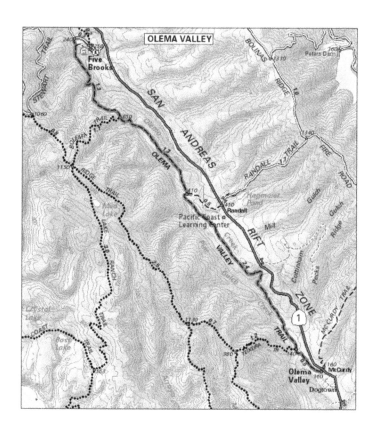

OLEMA VALLEY

OLEMA VALLEY TRAIL

**From Five Brooks Trailhead to Dogtown/Olema Valley
Trailhead is 5.5 miles one way with 400-foot elevation gain**

A gorge formed by earthquake action along the
San Andreas Fault, Olema Valley extends some 10
miles south from the town of Olema to Bolinas
Lagoon. The pastoral valley is bounded by Bolinas
Ridge and Inverness Ridge.

Highway 1 passes through Olema Valley and
motorists get views of grazing cattle, Victorian
houses and the lovely lands preserved in two national
parks—Golden Gate National Recreation Area and
Point Reyes National Seashore. Olema Valley lies
within the boundaries of GGNRA, though administered by Point Reyes National Seashore.

Olema Valley Trail follows the rift zone of the
San Andreas Fault, traverses about half the Olema
Valley and brings hikers close-up views of its beau-
ties. The trail extends from the Five Brooks Trailhead
to the Olema Valley Trailhead.

Because of its popularity with mountain bikers and horseback riders, The Trailmaster suggests taking this hike as a one-way with a car shuttle rather than an out-and-back. Note: the mile of trail nearest the Olema Valley Trailhead is sometimes overgrown and crowded by abundant poison oak.

DIRECTIONS: From Highway 1, some 9 miles north of Stinson Beach and 3.5 miles south of Olema, turn west at the signed turnoff for Five Brooks and drive 0.25 mile to the large parking area.

THE HIKE: Sometimes a hike begins like this— you must hike north before you can hike south. Join Stewart Trail for 0.3 mile, passing a pond that supports populations of resident and migratory birds.

At the junction with Olema Trail, turn left, then right, descending into a mixed forest of Douglas fir, oak and bay. Nearly a mile out, the path crosses a bridge and begins to climb, moderately and steeply to junction Bolema Trail.

Bear leftward on Olema Valley Trail and descend to a small meadow and narrows. The trail meanders from grassland to woodland, and descends to meet Randall Trail at the 3.1-mile mark.

Continue your southeast passage on Olema Valley Trail. A half-mile later, you'll pass a national park residence, then travel through forest and meadow to a crossing at Pine Creek, 4.7 miles into the hike. No bridge here, but the water is usually fairly shallow.

Continue on what is usually the most vegetation-impaired part of the trail. Beware of poison oak. Hike past a junction with Teixeira Trail at the 5-mile mark, cross another creek and hike a last half mile on overgrown trail to the Olema Valley Trailhead in Dogtown.

Olema Valley: Peaceful pathways, two national parks, and a pastoral landscape dotted with cows.

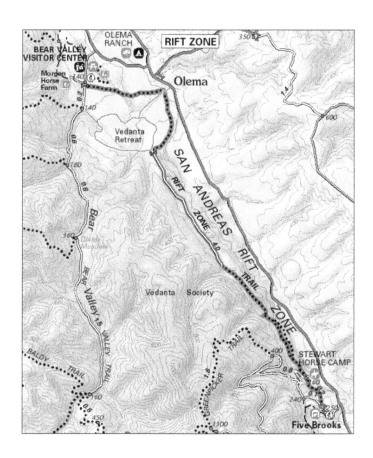

RIFT ZONE

RIFT ZONE TRAIL

From Five Brooks to Olema is 4 miles one way; to Bear Valley Visitor Center is 4.6 miles one way with 200-foot elevation gain

The word "rift," whether describing a fissure in a friendship or lateral movement along an earthquake fault, does not have pleasant associations; therefore it might be with some surprise that the hiker discovers pastoral beauty and tranquility along the Rift Zone Trail.

The path is accurately named—it follows the San Andreas Rift Zone—but the terrain traversed appears less like a textbook example of plate tectonics than a gentle montage of meadows, pastures, woodlands and wildflowers.

The trail traverses land belonging to the Vedanta Society, a Hindu-oriented religious organization. Observe posted rules and remember to close all livestock gates.

Arrange a car shuttle and make this a one-way journey on mostly level trail. End at Bear Valley Visitor Center, which has full facilities. Another option is hiking one-way or round trip to the hamlet of Olema. A short spur trail leads to Point Reyes Seashore Lodge and tiny Olema at the junction of Highway 1 and Sir Francis Drake Highway. A little store/deli and a restaurant/tavern offer food and beverages.

The trail is best hiked in autumn, winter or spring. In summer, the path is quite dusty and receives heavy use by horseback riders. Beware of yellowjackets.

DIRECTIONS: From Highway 1, some 9 miles north of Stinson Beach and 3.5 miles south of Olema, turn west at the signed turnoff for Five Brooks and drive 0.25 mile to the large parking area.

THE HIKE: The mill pond near the trailhead was created in the 1950s by a lumber company that floated logs across it to a sawmill. When the national seashore was established in 1962, the practice of chopping-down Douglas fir was halted. Look for venerable firs that escaped the loggers and many young firs that are replacing the original forest.

Walk west on the main road (trail) toward Inverness Ridge and in 0.3 mile reach Stewart Horse camp. Descend to join signed Rift Zone Trail among clusters of California hazelnut, pass a trail that leads to Firtop, and soon cross a branch of Olema Creek.

After a mellow mile, the path switchbacks up to Vedanta Society land. You then begin two miles of travel along an old farm road. The closed canopy of the moist forest (ferns, fir, bay trees) wraps the hiker in a quiet cocoon.

Head around a corral, pass through a pasture grazed by Black Angus cattle, then walk northwest across a wide field toward a windbreak of cypress and eucalyptus that lines the road to the Vedanta Society retreat. As you cross a meadow, look eastward for a short connector trail that leads to the back of Point Reyes Seashore Lodge.

Rift Zone Trail crosses a pasture behind the lodge, passes through a gate, ascends a knoll, and drops into a pretty little meadow extending to Bear Valley. Trail's end is a junction with Bear Valley Trail close to Bear Valley Visitor Center.

*Watch for black-tailed deer and other wildlife
in the heart of the park*

EVERY TRAIL TELLS A STORY.

II
Bear Valley &
Limantour

HIKE ON.

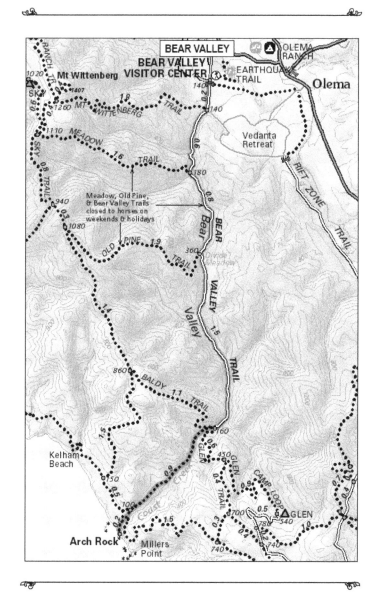

Meadow, Old Pine, & Bear Valley Trails closed to horses on weekends & holidays

BEAR VALLEY

BEAR VALLEY VISITOR CENTER

Mt Wittenberg

Olema

OLEMA RANCH

EARTHQUAKE TRAIL

Vedanta Retreat

Divide Meadow

Kelham Beach

Arch Rock

Millers Point

GLEN

GLEN

Camp Loop

GLEN

Coast

Bear Valley

Coast Creek

Bear Valley

Bear Valley Trail

From Bear Valley Visitor Center to Divide Meadow is 3.2 miles round trip; to trail's end is 8.2 miles round trip; to Kelham Beach is 10 miles round trip

What's not to like about a fairly flat footpath that leads through lovely forest and across wide meadows to the sea? No wonder Bear Valley Trail, a former wagon road, is one of the most popular paths (perhaps the *most* popular) in the national seashore.

The trail (about 75 percent of it a wide dirt road) begins at the park's main visitor center and meanders along Bear Creek and amidst a mixed Douglas fir forest to Divide Meadow, and then along Coast Creek to the coast.

For more than 50 years, the destination for this hike was Arch Rock, an overlook point above the arch. However the arch collapsed—a victim of relentless cliff erosion, and Arch Rock Trail (0.2 mile), which leads to a vista of what remains of the arch, is closed.

With Arch Rock out of the picture, we can satisfy our urge to hike to the sea by heading north 0.9 mile on Coast Trail to reach Kelham Beach.

DIRECTIONS: Bear Valley Visitor Center is located just outside the town of Olema, 35 slow and curving miles north of San Francisco on Highway 1. A quicker route is by Highway 101, exiting on Sir Francis Drake Boulevard, and traveling 20 miles to Olema. Turn right on Coast Highway 1, proceed 0.1 mile, then turn left on Bear Valley Road, which leads 0.4 mile to parking for the Point Reyes National Seashore Visitor Center and the trailhead.

THE HIKE: Bear Valley Trail leads through open meadow and, after 0.2 mile, passes a junction with Mt. Wittenberg Trail, which ascends Mt. Wittenberg.

Beyond this junction, the trail enters a forest of Bishop pine and Douglas fir. Your path is alongside Bear Valley Creek. Notice that the creek flows north, in the opposite direction of Coast Creek, which accompanies Bear Valley Trail from Divide Meadow to the sea. This strange drainage pattern is one more example of how the mighty San Andreas Fault can shape the land.

A half-mile along, pass a junction with Meadow Trail and, after almost another mile of travel, arrive at Divide Meadow, 1.6 miles from the trailhead. Well-named Divide Meadow divides Bear Valley Creek from Coast Creek. Bordered by Douglas fir, the meadow is a fine place for a picnic, as well as being a popular destination/

turnaround point for many hikers. It's also, literally, the hike's high point (about 360 feet above sea level).

Re-entering the forest, shady Bear Valley Trail continues another 1.5 mile to a junction with northbound Baldy Trail and southbound Glen Trail. At the 3.2- mile mark, Bear Valley Trail narrows from road to footpath (from which bikes are banned), and heads for the coast in the shade of Douglas fir.

Four miles along, the trail ends at a junction with Coast Trail. (If Arch Rock Trail is re-opened, you can join the path as it crosses through coastal scrub and arrives at an open meadow on the precipitous bluffs above sea stacks and the remnants of Arch Rock. This is an overlook point with no official beach access.)

To get to the beach, hike north on Coast Trail. In 0.9 mile, reach Kelham Beach Trail and follow this path 500 feet or so to Kelham Beach.

Divide Meadow, a highlight, the hike's high point, and popular destination for a short hike.

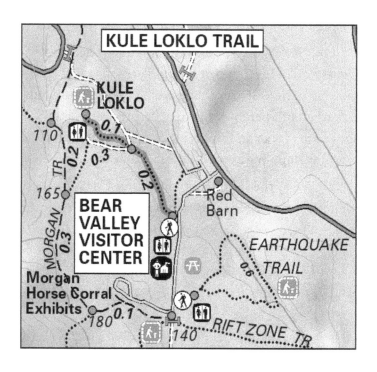

KULE LOKLO

KULE LOKLO TRAIL

0.8 mile round trip with 50-foot elevation gain

Kule Loklo ("Bear Valley"), a replica of a Coast Miwok village, illustrates how the region's indigenous people lived, indeed flourished in this land of abundant natural resources. Experience the village on a fine self-guided trail or ranger-led walk.

DIRECTIONS: See Bear Valley/Earthquake Trail hike descriptions. Kule Loklo Trailhead is located at the north end of the Bear Valley Visitor Center parking lot.

THE HIKE: The trail, a dirt fire road, makes a mellow ascent amidst Douglas fir, soon emerging in a clearing that affords a look down on Bear Valley, its meadows and visitor center. Meandering over to a eucalyptus grove, you bear right on the path to reach the village.

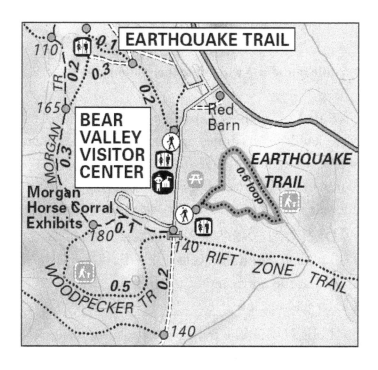

EARTHQUAKE TRAIL

110

MORGAN TR

0.1

0.2

0.3

0.2

165

BEAR
VALLEY
VISITOR
CENTER

0.3

Red
Barn

EARTHQUAKE

TRAIL

0.6 loop

Morgan
Horse Corral
Exhibits

0.1

180

0.1

140

RIFT ZONE TRAIL

WOODPECKER TR

0.5

0.2

140

All About Earthquakes
Earthquake Trail

0.6 mile

Earthquake Trail uses old photographs and other displays to explain the seismic forces unleashed by the great 1906 San Francisco earthquake. This well-done and entertaining geology lesson is particularly relevant because most of the land west of the San Andreas Fault Zone is within boundaries of Point Reyes National Seashore.

Plates forming the earth's crust do not always creep quietly past each other. In 1906 they clashed violently, and the result was California's worst natural disaster. During the great quake, Point Reyes was shoved 16.4 feet to the northwest. A cow barn, located near the park rangers' headquarters, was ripped in two. A corner of the barn stayed on the foundation and the rest was carried sixteen feet away.

The San Andreas Fault is long (780 miles), narrow (one mile) and deep (20 miles). For obvious reasons, the fault is much-studied by scientists and as a result much research is available to share with the public. Surely a hike along Earthquake Trail is one of the most interesting ways to learn more about this great maker and shaker of continents.

Paved and fully accessible for all visitors, the nearly flat trail is an engaging experience for all ages. On this memorable nature trail view creeks and fences that were rearranged by the 1906 quake.

And Earthquake Trail is more than an earth science lesson. The path also offers a friendly intro to the parkland's meadow and woodland communities. Even the most time-pressed tourist will enjoy walking the trail.

DIRECTIONS: Bear Valley Visitor Center is located just outside the town of Olema, 35 slow and curving miles north of San Francisco on Highway 1. A quicker route is by Highway 101, exiting on Sir Francis Drake Boulevard, and traveling 20 miles to Olema. Turn right on Coast Highway 1, proceed 0.1 mile, then turn left on Bear Valley Road, which leads 0.4 mile to parking for the Point Reyes National Seashore Visitor Center. Earthquake Trail begins at the southeast corner of the Bear Valley Picnic Area, right across the road from the Bear Valley Visitor Center.

THE HIKE: Study the interpretive panel of the San Andreas Fault in relief and walk into the meadow. Earthquake Trail soon forks: arrows on the pavement suggest you bear left (east).

View photos of the San Francisco Earthquake and follow the trail amidst tangles of blackberry to an oak woodland and crosses a bridge over a branch of Olema Creek.

The path curves south and passes more interpretive panels. Be sure to read the story of the cow caught in…well, I won't spoil the colorful tale. Suffice it to say that it's the best-known urban legend—rural legend, really—of Point Reyes.

And finally, make sure you walk the short side trail to inspect a 16-foot break in the old fence line; this is the showstopper, a memorable illustration of the power of the quake of 1906 and quakes to come.

Bear Valley Visitor Center: Great place to learn all about Point Reyes, and trailhead for many excellent hikes.

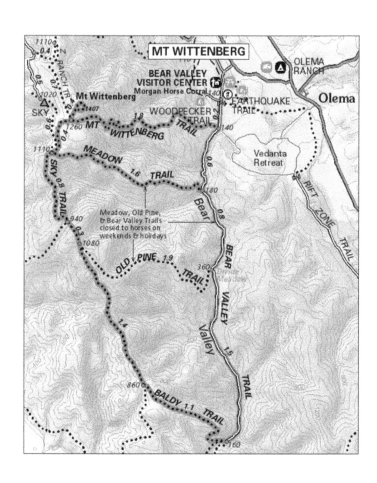

MT. WITTENBERG

MT. WITTENBERG, SKY, MEADOW, TRAILS

**From Bear Valley Trailhead to Mt. Wittenberg summit is
4.7 miles round trip with 1,300-foot elevation gain**

Highest summit on Point Reyes National Seashore, 1,407-foot Mt. Wittenberg offers sweeping vistas of the entire Point Reyes Peninsula: Tomales Bay, Olema Valley, Bolinas Ridge. On clear days, look for distant Mt. St. Helena and Mt. Diablo.

Don't change your hiking plans on a gray overcast day. Even wrapped in fog, the slopes of Wittenberg, covered as they are with hanging mosses, colorful lichen and ferns have an enchanting forest primeval-like quality. I've enjoyed hiking the mountains as much or more in foul weather as fair.

From the summit, join Sky Trail along Inverness Ridge, then choose return route: via Meadow Trail for a 5.4 mile round trip hike; via Old Pine Trail for a 6.6 miles round trip hike; via Baldy Trail for 8.6 miles round trip.

DIRECTIONS: Bear Valley Visitor Center is located just outside the town of Olema, 35 miles north of San Francisco on Highway 1. Turn left on Bear Valley Road, and drive 0.4 mile to parking for the Point Reyes National Seashore Visitor Center and the trailhead.

THE HIKE: Begin on Bear Valley Trail and in 0.2 mile reach a right-forking junction at a large bay tree with signed Mt. Wittenberg Trail. With sword ferns pointing the way, the path climbs past a mixed forest of tanbark oak and Douglas fir. After gaining more than a thousand feet in elevation, reach the ridgecrest and a junction with Z-Ranch Trail at the two-mile mark (and about 1,200 feet in elevation).

Join the rightward path (Wittenberg Summit Trail) for a 0.3-mile climb across grassland through patches of woodland, and curving around to the top of Mt. Wittenberg. The path peters out in tall grass. Concentrate on your surroundings; the summit, especially when mist enshrouded, can be disorienting.

Enjoy clear-day views south and east including plenty of Point Reyes and Mt. Tamalpais; trees on the summit screen the views north and west.

Retrace your steps 0.3 mile on the Wittenberg Summit Trail back to the junction.

For a mellow, 1.5-mile descent back to Bear Valley, join east-trending Meadow Trail, cross a wide

meadow and get vistas across the peninsula to mighty
Mt. Tam. The path drops rapidly off Inverness Ridge,
descends past bay trees and Douglas fir to a footbridge crossing Bear Valley Creek and a junction
with Bear Valley Trail

For a longer return from the junction, continue
on Sky Trail, a dirt road. Travel south a mile through
a Douglas fir forest and past a variety of berry bushes
to meet Old Pine Trail, another easy way back to
Bear Valley. This trail descends 1.9 miles through a
long meadow and past a grove of Bishop pine.

For an even longer return, continue on Sky Trail
and descend along forested Inverness Ridge another
1.4 mile to face "Baldy," a 1,034-foot rock knob.
Baldy Trail drops a mile to Bear Valley; it's three
miles back to the trailhead.

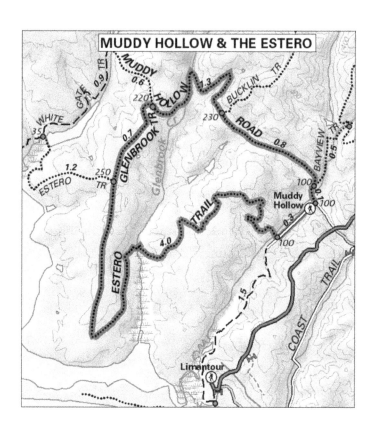

MUDDY HOLLOW & THE ESTERO

Muddy Hollow & The Estero

Muddy Hollow Road, Glenbrook, Estero, Muddy Hollow Trails

From Muddy Hollow around Estero to Limantour Beach and return via Limantour Road is a 7.2-mile loop with a 200-foot elevation gain

Limantour Road leads to Point Reyes Hostel and makes a beeline to the beach. It also delivers visitors to one of the national seashore's most obscure and least-developed trailheads. Muddy Hollow Trailhead is the departure point for some hiker-customized loops that tour hill and dale, beach and estero.

Muddy Hollow is indeed muddy and was probably even more so when this was dairy land and lots of cows tromped through the hollow.

DIRECTIONS: From Olema, drive north on Highway 1 for 0.1 miles and turn left on Bear Valley Road. Drive 1.8 miles and turn left on Limantour

Road. Continue 5.75 miles to a signed dirt road. Turn right and drive 0.25 miles to the trailhead.

THE HIKE: Walk north on Muddy Hollow Road/Trail. The wide path crosses a creek and in 0.1 miles junctions with Bayview Trail. Continue on Muddy Hollow Road. Reminders of the devastating 1995 Vision Fire are present in the form of blackened trees. As the road ascends, look leftward (to the south) for a trio of ponds.

At the 0.9-mile mark the trail passes a junction with northbound Bucklin Trail (which ascends to Point Reyes Hill). Stick with Muddy Hollow Road, which descends, crosses Glenbrook Creek, and ascends to intersect signed Glenbrook Trail, 2.2 miles from the trailhead.

Join Glenbrook Trail, heading south on what has never been the best-maintained of trails. Watch for rabbits bounding through the blue-eyed grass. After 0.7 miles, the trail ends at a 3-way junction with Estero Trail.

Continue straight (south) on Estero Trail. If you're looking for solitude, this next stretch (4 miles) definitely delivers it; the times I've hiked it, other hikers have been few or nonexistent. The mostly level trail leads about 1.2 miles to within spitting distance (OK, that's an exaggeration, more like to within a quarter mile) of Limantour Spit. Listen for the boisterous barking of the seals that haul-out on the spit.

Estero Trail bends east, then north, traveling about 0.8 miles to a bridge over Glenbrook Creek. The trail then weaves east through the alder-lined watershed and amidst tangles of nettle and salmon-berries, and soon ascends to higher and drier ground clad in the coastal scrub community.

Continuing northeasterly on open, grass and scrub-covered slopes to the crest of the hill, it then turns east and follows a gently contoured route, winding down to a stream crossing over a wooden bridge within sight of a junction with a wide dirt road. Turn left (northeast) and follow the level road 0.3 miles back to the trailhead.

Thank you YCC workers and the many others who maintain Muddy Hollow Road Trail and all the other park pathways.

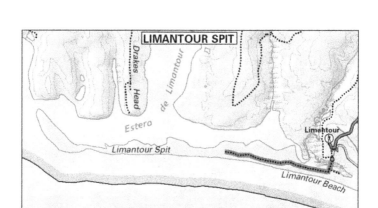

LIMANTOUR BEACH

LIMANTOUR SPIT TRAIL

**From Limantour Trailhead to end of Limantour Spit is
5.6 miles round trip**

Many coast walkers claim Limantour Beach is
the Bay Area's best for walking. Sandy Limantour
Beach invites long walks, Limantour Estero attracts
bird watchers to its shores, and long Limantour Sand
Spit offers splendidly scenic passageway between the
ocean and the estero.

Curious sand spit sojourners want to know:
Where does the spit come from? Pacific waves, aris-
ing from the northwest, hammer the head of Point
Reyes; greatly deflected, the waves end up approach-
ing land from the south. This odd swell contributes
sand to Limantour Spit.

Along Limantour Spit Trail, hikers get an egret's-
eye view of pickleweed- and eelgrass-fringed Limantour Estero. Black brandts, pelicans and many more
bird species feed and rest at the estero. Sea lions and

harbor seals often haul-out near the western end of the spit.

Feel fortunate about what we don't see. Limantour Spit Trail was once Limantour Drive, the way to a subdivision that began construction just prior to the establishment of Point Reyes National Seashore in 1962. The National Park Service removed the half dozen houses that were built.

In 1841, Jose Yves Limantour, sailed from Mexico with a ship loaded with luxury goods and ran aground on the spit that now bears his name. Limantour's place in history, however, comes from his shady real estate dealings.

Claiming to have received thousands of acres worth of land grants during Mexico's governance of California, Limantour sold much of "his" land (in downtown San Francisco no less) before the federal

Limantour Beach earns votes for
"Best Beach Hike"

government determined his documents to be fraudulent and he fled to Mexico.

Whether along San Diego Bay, Morro Bay or Drakes Bay, spit-walking is a special experience because the walker is simultaneously treated to both Pacific and estuary environments and ever-changing patterns of water meeting land.

DIRECTIONS: From Olema, drive north on Highway 1 for 0.1 mile and turn left on Bear Valley Road. Drive 1.8 miles and turn left on Limantour Road. Continue to road's end at a parking area.

THE HIKE: From the parking lot, follow the gravel path 0.25 mile to Limantour Beach. Bypass Muddy Hollow Trailhead and fork right on Limantour Spit Trail. The trail serves up equal measures of Pacific and estero views as it skirts Estero de Limantour.

After about 1.3 miles, the path peters out, and most hikers wander over to the beach. (The intrepid can, however, trek over the tops of the tall dunes with the reward of superlative views.)

The second leg of the hike (1.5 miles) is a wonderfully wild excursion—particularly after a winter storm when there's apt to be all manner of flotsam and jetsam cast upon the beach. From spit's end you'll witness a meeting of Estero de Limantour and Drakes Estero.

Call of the wild: Bull elephant seal bellowing

EVERY TRAIL TELLS A STORY.

III

Sir Francis Drake Highway

HIKE ON.

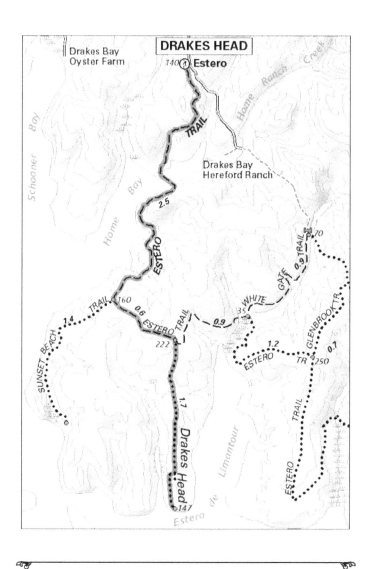

Drakes Bay
Oyster Farm

DRAKES HEAD

140 ▲ **Estero**

Schooner Bay

Home Bay

TRAIL

Home Ranch Creek

Drakes Bay
Hereford Ranch

2.5

ESTERO

0.9 TRAIL

70

WHITE GATE

SUNSET BEACH TRAIL

160

1.4

0.6 ESTERO TRAIL

35

0.9

GLENBROOK TR.

0.7

222

1.2

ESTERO TR 250

1.1

Drakes Head

ESTERO TRAIL

147

Estero

Limantour

Estero de

DRAKES ESTERO

ESTERO AND DRAKES HEAD TRAILS

From Estero Trailhead to Drakes Head is 9.4 miles round trip with 500-foot elevation gain

This memorable hike over old ranch roads on the western slope of Inverness Ridge visits Drakes *Estero* (Spanish for estuary), where wildlife is abundant. Great blue herons, willets, godwits, sanderlings, sandpipers and many more shorebirds feed along the mudflats. Harbor seals and sea lions often swim into the estero and bask on its beaches.

The Trailmaster has had the pleasure of guiding visitors from across the U.S. and around Europe on this trail, and it's one long remembered by all who hike it. If time-short, take the 1.2-mile walk as far as the bridge across Home Bay.

DIRECTIONS: From Highway 1 in Olema (where there's a well-marked turnoff for the Point Reyes National Seashore Bear Valley Visitor Center), drive two miles north and veer left onto Sir Francis

Drake Highway. Follow the highway 7.5 miles to Estero Road. Turn left and drive a mile to the Estero parking area and signed trailhead.

THE HIKE: Estero Trail, an old ranch road, climbs gently across pastoral grasslands. As you climb look over your left shoulder and admire Inverness Ridge, highlighted by, from west to east, Mt. Vision, Point Reyes Hill, and Mt. Wittenberg. The trail turns left and, at about a half mile from the trailhead, passes a stand of Monterey pine, once the nucleus of a Christmas tree farm.

At 1.2 miles, the path crosses a causeway, which divides Home Bay from a pond. Large numbers of shorebirds frequent the mudflats of Home Bay. The many fingers of Drake's Estero are patrolled by canvasbacks, ruddy ducks and American wigeons. For wildlife-watching convenience, benches are built into the bridge.

The trail (a rutted track indeed) ascends lupine-dotted slopes and offers good views of Home Bay shores and its many habitués. Look for deer, both native black-tailed, or the "imported" white fallow, browsing the grassy ridges. After a 0.25-mile climb, pass through a gate and continue a moderately aggressive ascent above Drakes Estero. The ascent brings vistas of the estero, as well as Creamery Bay and Schooner Bays.

About 2.5 miles from the trailhead, reach a signed junction. (Sunset Beach Trail heads straight (southwest) well above the estero for more than a mile before dropping to a rocky beach with substantial tide pools, 1.4 miles from its junction with Estero Trail.)

Estero Trail climbs steeply for 0.25 mile to a cattle tank and signed junction that guides you hard right through a turnstile. Small arrow signs keep you on the trail, which parallels a fence along an often-grazed pasture. At the 3.1-mile mark, junction Drakes Head Trail.

Head right (south) over fields. Estero de Limantour comes into view. A mile down the trail, look for a wooden post and prepare for a sudden right turn.

The trail continues to Drakes Head, about 150-feet above the water. Experienced hikers can pick their way down the extremely steep Head east to Estero de Limantour.

Drakes Estero, the most likely landing spot of Sir Francis Drake on the coast of North America in 1579.

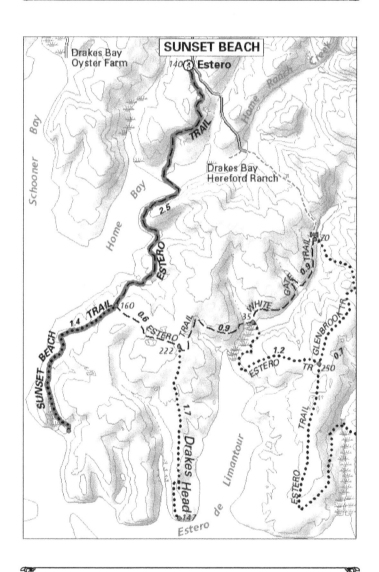

Drakes Bay
Oyster Farm

SUNSET BEACH
140 Estero

Schooner Bay

Home Bay

Home Ranch Creek

Drakes Bay
Hereford Ranch

TRAIL

2.5

ESTERO

270

0.9

GATE

TRAIL

GLENBROOK TR

SUNSET-BEACH TRAIL

1.4

160

0.6

ESTERO TRAIL

222

WHITE

35

0.9

1.2

ESTERO

TR

250

0.7

ESTERO TRAIL

1.7

Drakes Head

147

Estero de Limantour

SUNSET BEACH

ESTERO AND SUNSET BEACH TRAILS

From Estero Trailhead to Sunset Beach is 8 miles round trip with 200-foot elevation gain

Located west of Drakes Head and extending inside the mouth of Drakes Estero, Sunset Beach, narrow and mostly rocky, is noted for its tide pools, some of the richest in Point Reyes National Seashore. The reason for this abundant intertidal life (crabs, anemones, mussels, sea stars, urchins and sponges) is a prime location at the intersection of estuary and open ocean. (Time your hike to arrive at low tide.)

The hike to Sunset Beach and the one to Drakes Head share a common trailhead and a common beginning—splendid Estero Trail, offering hikers the opportunity to observe the abundant wildlife around Drakes *Estero*, Spanish for estuary.

About 2.6 miles from Estero Trailhead, the paths diverge, with Estero Trail curving west and the trail to Sunset Beach continuing along Drakes Estero.

Despite its name, Sunset Beach Trail is not a beach trail, but rather a hillside path that delivers fine vistas of Drakes Estero, Drakes Beach, Bull Point and the Pacific Ocean.

DIRECTIONS: From Highway 1 in Olema, proceed two miles north and veer left onto Sir Francis Drake Highway. Follow the highway 7.5 miles to Estero Road. Turn left and drive a mile to Estero parking and trailhead.

THE HIKE: Estero Trail, an old ranch road, climbs gently across pastoral grasslands. As you climb get vistas of Inverness Ridge, highlighted by, from west to east, Mt. Vision, Point Reyes Hill, and Mt. Wittenberg.

The trail turns to the left and, at about a half mile from the trailhead, passes a stand of Monterey pine, once a Christmas tree farm.

At 1.2 miles, the path crosses a causeway, which divides Home Bay from a pond. Even the most casual birder will sight large numbers of shorebirds in the mudflats of Home Bay. The many fingers of Drake's Estero are patrolled by canvasbacks, ruddy ducks and American wigeons.

The trail (a rutted track indeed) ascends lupine-dotted slopes and offers good views of Home Bay shores and its many habitués. Look for deer, either the native black-tailed or the "imported" white fallow browsing the grassy ridges. After a 0.25-mile climb, pass through a gate and continue a moderately-aggressive ascent, higher and higher above Drakes Estero. Enjoy vistas of the estero, as well as Creamery Bay and Schooner Bays.

About 2.5 miles from the trailhead, reach a signed junction and join Sunset Beach Trail as it heads straight (southwest) on a gentle descent, well above the estero. The trail traverses grassland and passes blackberry patches. (Keep on the main trail; it's cut with many a cattle path.)

Sunset Beach Trail travels between two low hills and, about 0.9 mile from its junction with Estero Trail, passes to the left of a lagoon. Meandering amidst coyote brush and, nearer the water, pickle-weed, the path levels. Near trail's end is the rocky beach, located below a substantial headland by the mouth of Drakes Estero.

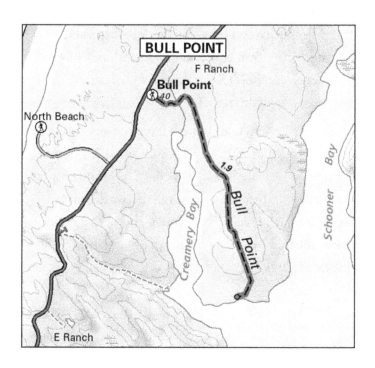

BULL POINT

F Ranch

Bull Point

North Beach

40

1.9

Bull Point

Creamery Bay

Schooner Bay

E Ranch

Bull Point

Bull Point Trail

From Drake Highway to Drakes Estero is 3.8 miles round trip with 100-foot elevation gain

With its "green pastures" and "still waters" the walk across Bull Point has a few highlights that recall the 23rd Psalm.

Herefords and Black Angus graze the green pastures of the headlands. This is cow country, and has been since the 1850s. Schooners maneuvered into Drakes Estero, took on a cargo of fine butter, and returned to San Francisco, a ready market for dairy products produced on Point Reyes.

The still waters around Bull Point include Creamery Bay, Schooner Bay and Drakes Estero. Bring your field glasses for birding, as well as to watch for deer browsing the headlands, and for harbor seals and sea lions, which often swim into the estero.

Bull Point Trail traverses a wide headland between two arms of Drakes Estero—Schooner Bay and Creamery Bay. The mostly level path (an old farm road) crosses the grassy headlands and offers the opportunity to glimpse lots of wildlife, as well as plenty of grazing cows. The trail crosses F Ranch so figure on crossing paths with some cattle; just be patient, and let them pass.

Bull Point and vicinity looks like a drowsy slice of pre-Industrial Revolution England, but it was a much busier place in the 19th century. Thriving ranches, a post office and a bustling schooner landing on Schooner Bay combined to put the area on the map. The schooners carried Point Reyes Peninsula butter to eager San Francisco buyers.

DIRECTIONS: From Highway 1 in Olema, turn west on Bear Valley Road and drive 2.2 miles to meet Sir Francis Drake Highway. Turn left and proceed 10.8 miles to the signed parking area on the left side of the highway.

THE HIKE: For the first hundred yards or so, Bull Point Trail (an old ranch road) is rather cow-trampled and a bit hard to follow. The path crosses a pasture and travels 0.3 mile to a cattle gate. The trail (lengths of which are retiring ranch road), curves south and ascends gently along Creamery Bay. Watch for the seals that haul-out on the bay mudflats.

The path curves south into the middle of Bull Point. Mostly level, the route is over country open and all but treeless—a melancholy scene on an overcast day. The path reaches its high point—such as it is—at 100 feet in elevation at about 1.1 miles from the trailhead. When presented with a choice, opt for the double track—as opposed to the more narrow cattle paths.

Nearing the water, observe Schooner Bay to your left, Creamery Bay to the right. Those poles thrusting up from the muddy bottom of Schooner Bay belong to oyster farmers: many a mollusk is harvested from these waters.

Bull Point Trail ends at the edge of a low bluff. A faint trail leads down to a narrow rock beach.

DRAKES BEACH

DRAKES BEACH TRAIL

2 to 3 miles round trip

This south-facing beach, with generally gentle surf, is considered one of the safest and most family-friendly on Point Reyes. Drakes Beach is out of the prevailing wind so it's warmer than, say, the region's west-facing beaches.

The amenities are great for a day at the beach: clean restrooms, showers to get the sand off you, a café, and plenty of free parking. Drakes Beach is the site of the Point Reyes annual sand sculpture contest that takes place in late August.

Historical controversy as thick as the summer fog envelops Drakes Bay. Is this really the place where English explorer Francis Drake landed his Golden Hinde in 1579? Or did he come ashore at another location in San Francisco Bay? Bodega Bay? Tomales Bay?

Drake-ologists, academic and amateur, have debated about who landed where and why for years.

Sir Francis Drake: exactly where on Point Reyes he landed on June 17, 1579, has been the subject of much spirited debate.

Certainly the tall white cliffs back of Drakes Beach match the description recorded in Drake's journal, and are convincing evidence advanced by the pro-Drakes Bay majority.

Believer or not, you'll enjoy a saunter along Drakes Bay. South-facing Drakes Beach is more sheltered from the wind than the national seashore's western-facing beaches and is fringed by a bay instead of the open ocean; this adds up to an altogether calmer walking experience. Drakes Beach is accessible for two miles or so to the west; most of its eastern stretch is accessible only at low tide.

For an excellent overview of the great Drake debate, check out the excellent interpretive exhibits at the Ken C. Patrick Visitor Center, housed in a handsome redwood building with a beach-facing deck. The park service does an excellent job of discussing Drake's voyage in its many cultural and political manifestations.

Observe a moment of silence for visitor center namesake Ranger Patrick, the first national park service ranger killed in the field. Deer poachers shot him on Mt. Vision.

Drakes Beach Café is a park concession and the only food service within the national seashore boundary, so the hungry hiker might fear the worst. However, visitors from both the Bay Area and faraway, praise the quality of food served at the café.

Short hiking trails traverse the bluffs and offer good views. Get a great overview of Drakes Bay from the Peter Behr Overlook, located 0.25 mile by paved path south of the visitor center.

DIRECTIONS: From the hamlet of Olema, head 0.1 mile north on Highway 1 to Bear Valley Road. Turn left and proceed 2.25 miles to Sir Francis Drake Highway. Turn left and drive 13.5 miles to the signed turnoff for Drakes Beach. Turn left and go 1.5 miles to road's end and the large parking area near the visitor center.

THE HIKE: You can wander east past a little lagoon and continue (best at low tide) toward Drakes Estero. Elephant seals have been known to haul-out on Drakes Beach.

The way southwest is an enjoyable saunter of two miles or so.

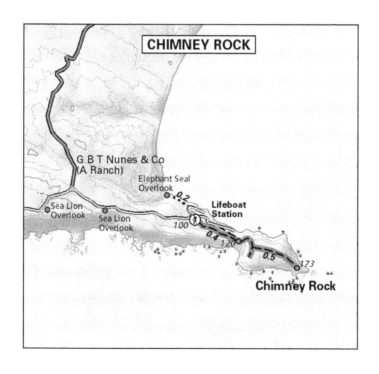

CHIMNEY ROCK

CHIMNEY ROCK TRAIL

To Chimney Rock Overlook is 1.8 miles round trip

So compelling is Point Reyes Lighthouse, most visitors don't bother with the walk to Chimney Rock Overlook, which offers a panoramic view nearly equal to that of the lighthouse. You'll travel a spring wildflower-lined path, glimpsing an old U.S. Coast Guard Lifeboat Station. While you might not be able to discern which offshore rock resembles a chimney, you will be able to view the coastline all the way to San Francisco on a clear day.

In spring, expect lots of wildflowers, including lupine, poppies and Douglas iris. Experts have counted five-dozen species.

From December to February, don't miss the short walk to Elephant Seal Overlook. The enormous, boisterous creatures re-colonized isolated Point Reyes beaches in the early 1980s. This is one of the best places to safely observe them. From January through

May, observe migrating gray whales on their north-ward migration.

Naturalists consider the Point Reyes Headlands, which extend about 3.5 miles from Chimney Rock to the Point Reyes Lighthouse, among the most important rocky shoreline habitats on the peninsula. Crucial habitat for invertebrates, marine mammals and seabirds, the granitic promontory is also known for its abundance of seastars (starfish), including the 20-rayed star or sunstar.

A short walk leads to the Point Reyes Lifesaving Station, which was constructed in 1927 and continued in operation until 1968. Notwithstanding the mighty beacon of nearby Point Reyes Lighthouse, many shipwrecks occurred and there were many calls for the Coast Guard, whose brave men saved dozens of lives. The National Park Service restored the station and it was declared a National Historic Landmark in 1990.

DIRECTIONS: From Highway 101 in Olema, drive north a short distance, then turn left on Sir Francis Drake Highway and proceed 17.5 miles to the signed turnoff for Chimney Rock. Turn left and drive another mile to the parking area and signed trailhead.

THE HIKE: From the parking lot, follow the trail across the grassy cliffs. Savor a view of the sparkling white cliffs back of Drakes Beach. Detour over to an overlook of Point Reyes Peninsula and, on especially clear days, the Farallon Islands.

Be extra careful around the cliff edges and along social trails off the main route of travel. There is no safe beach access.

Back on the main path, continue your wind-blown way to the cliff-top vista point. Sea stacks and the surging surf are part of the dramatic seascape, a lively combo of Drakes Bay and great Pacific. Many birds nest on and near Chimney Rock, including Western gulls, cormorants, pigeon guillemots and black oystercatchers.

From Chimney Rock, views nearly as good as those from the Point Reyes Lighthouse.

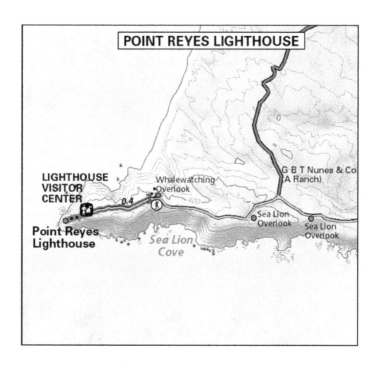

POINT REYES LIGHTHOUSE

LIGHTHOUSE
VISITOR
CENTER

Point Reyes
Lighthouse

Whalewatching
Overlook

Sea Lion
Cove

G B T Nunes & Co
(A Ranch)

Sea Lion
Overlook

Sea Lion
Overlook

0.4

TheTrailmaster.com

Point Reyes Lighthouse

To Lighthouse is 1 mile round trip with 400-foot elevation gain

Some lighthouses welcome sailors to port; some lighthouses warn them of danger. Point Reyes Lighthouse was most certainly built to warn vessels away from a treacherous coastline that was the death of many ships.

Congress voted construction funds for a light back in 1852 but legal tussles with coastal bluff landowners delayed installation until 1870. Meanwhile, many more ships ran aground.

From past experience, lighthouse keepers had learned that placing a light too high atop California's coastal cliffs diminished the light's fog-penetrating effectiveness; thus, the Point Reyes Lighthouse was built about halfway down the 600-foot bluffs.

The odd placement of the station greatly increased its construction costs, as well as the costs of supplying it during its century of service. Nasty weather, isolation from the world, and the relentless bellow of the foghorn made the lot of the lighthouse keeper a difficult one and contributed to drinking and discipline problems. Some keepers went outright bonkers.

The 16-sided lighthouse is anchored to the cliff with large bolts. The Fresnel lens was first lit in 1870. It's 24 panels revolve once every two minutes, producing a white flash for ships at sea every five seconds.

By some accounts, Point Reyes is the foggiest point on the Pacific Coast, and supposedly second only to Rhode Island's Nantucket Island in the entire U.S. A week or more can pass without any sun. When the foggy curtain lifts, however, the lighthouse

No visit to Point Reyes is complete without taking the short hike to the iconic lighthouse, built in 1870.

observation platform is a superb place from which to watch for migrating California gray whales. During the winter months, bring your binoculars and scan the horizon for the passing gentle giants.

Point Reyes is also one of the windiest points on the Pacific Coast. Sixty mile-per hour winds are common and winds of more than one hundred miles an hour have been recorded. The high winds mean: 1) That fog can be blown away pronto 2) Dress warmly and in layers 3) Use caution on the path and stairways leading to the lighthouse.

The lighthouse visitor center is open Thursday through Monday, 10 a.m. to 4:30 p.m., weather permitting. Inquire at the center about tours of the facility. My family, kids included have always enjoyed the enthusiastic interpretation of the lighthouse by rangers and docents.

DIRECTIONS: From Highway 1 in Olema, drive north a short distance, then turn left on Sir Francis Drake Highway and drive north 18.5 miles to road's end at the parking lot for Point Reyes Lighthouse.

THE HIKE: A path and 308 stairs (like walking up and down the staircase of a 25-story building) comprise the route to the lighthouse.

*McClure's Beach: Sea stacks and more
along an inspiring shore.*

EVERY TRAIL TELLS A STORY.

IV

Tomales Bay &
Pierce Point Road

HIKE ON.

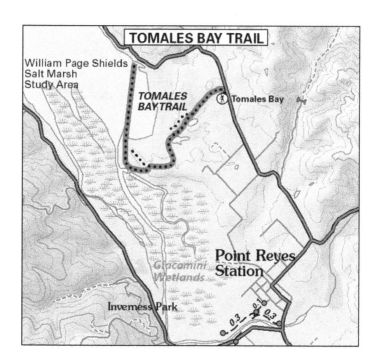

TOMALES BAY TRAIL

William Page Shields
Salt Marsh
Study Area

*TOMALES
BAY TRAIL*

Tomales Bay

*Giacomini
Wetlands*

**Point Reyes
Station**

Inverness Park

0.3   0.3   0.3

TOMALES BAY

TOMALES BAY TRAIL

From Highway 1 to Tomales Bay Levees is 2.6 miles round trip with 100-foot elevation gain

The trail name says it all. This is the way—a very pleasant way—to Tomales Bay.

Tomales Bay Trail usually escapes the notice of national seashore hikers for two reasons: 1) It's one of the very few footpaths on the east side of the bay and geographically isolated from the vast majority of land and trails on the Point Reyes Peninsula; 2) It's overshadowed by the similarly named and much more famous Tomales Point Trail that traverses the tule elk range on the northern tip of the peninsula.

Tomales Bay Trail offers glimpses into California's tumultuous geologic history. The bay is a submerged rift of the San Andreas Fault. Hikers walk atop the North American Plate (typified by mellow, rolling grassland) and look out at steep, wooded Inverness Ridge (characteristic terrain of the Pacific Plate).

Twelve miles long and a mile wide, the bay is a big-time bird habitat, hosting some one hundred species of water and shore birds. The bay's shallow waters (less than 10 feet deep in places along its southern end where the trail passes) nourish an assortment of clams, crabs and oysters, the latter raised commercially.

During the 1970s, the bay's southeastern shores attracted the attention of developers, who wished to purchase the 260-acre Elmer Matinelli Ranch and build a resort, golf course and housing development. The National Park Service purchased the property, however, and it has remained relatively pristine.

The National Park Service has plans to extend the trail to offer improved access to northern portions of this enclave to offer better access to the flooded flats and improved bird-watching opportunities.

DIRECTIONS: From the hamlet of Point Reyes Station, head north on Highway 1 for 1.5 miles to a signed National Park Service parking area on the west (left) side of the highway.

THE HIKE: From the north end of the parking area, join the westbound path and soon pass a large rock outcropping. Narrow trails branch from Tomales Bay Trail, but stick with the main path.

About 0.5 mile out, the trail travels near two, small cattail-fringed ponds patrolled by coots and mallards. Keep an eye out for egrets and red-wing blackbirds, frequently sighted near these ponds.

After the second pond, the path ascends a small hill, offers fine bay views, then descends to the marshy edge of Tomales Bay. Here you'll find some old levees and trestles—part of the right-of-way of the North Pacific Railroad that extended from Sausalito north to the town of Tomales and then up to the Sonoma County coast. The rail was active, under various owners, from the 1870s until 1933.

It's possible to hike north along the bay shore for a few hundred yards until a fence and intimidating clumps of poison oak halt the prudent hiker.

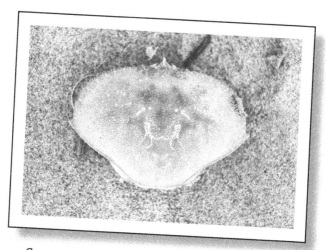

Crustacean alert: Many types of crabs live by the bay and along the peninsula's rocky shores.

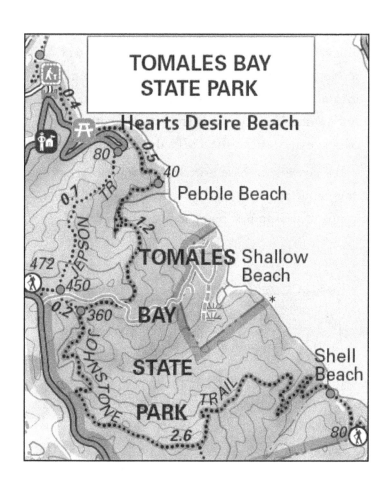

TOMALES BAY
STATE PARK

Hearts Desire Beach

Pebble Beach

TOMALES Shallow
Beach

BAY

STATE

PARK

Shell
Beach

Tomales Bay State Park

Johnstone and Jepson Trails

From Heart's Desire Beach to Jepson Memorial Grove is 3 miles round trip with 300-foot elevation gain; to Shell Beach is 8 miles round trip

Two lovely trails, named for a professor and a planner, explore Tomales Bay State Park. Botanist Willis Jepson, founder of the School of Forestry at the University of California, Berkeley, and author of the authoritative *Manual of the Flowering Plants of California*, is honored by the Jepson Trail.

Conservationist Bruce Johnstone, Marin County planner, and his wife Elsie, worked long and hard to preserve Tomales Bay and place part of it in a state park. Johnstone Trail leads bayside from Heart's Desire Beach to Shell Beach.

Bay Area walkers have a little secret: When fog smothers Point Reyes and San Francisco Bay, try heading for Tomales Bay State Park. The park has a microclimate, and often has sunny days and pleasant temperatures when other neighboring coastal locales are damp and cold.

DIRECTIONS: From the town of Inverness, follow Sir Francis Drake Boulevard to Pierce Point Road. Turn right and drive a half-mile to the entrance to Tomales Bay State Park. Follow signs to the large parking lot at Heart's Desire Beach.

THE HIKE: Signed Johnstone Trail departs from the south end of Heart's Desire Beach and immediately climbs into a moss-draped forest of oak, bay, madrone, and wax myrtle.

A half-mile of travel leads to Pebble Beach. At a trail junction, a short side trail goes straight down to Pebble Beach, but Johnstone Trail swings southwest and switchbacks up forested slopes. Ferns dot wetter areas of the coastal slope. The trail crosses a paved road and soon junctions.

To continue to Shell Beach, bear left with the Johnstone Trail. The trail detours around private property, and contours over the coastal slope at an elevation of about 500 feet. The path leads through Bishop pine and a lush understory of salal and huckleberry bushes. After a few miles, the trail descends through madrone and oak forest to Shell Beach.

Hikers content with looping back to Heart's Desire Beach via Jepson Trail will continue straight at the above-mentioned junction. Bishop pine, along with its similar-looking piney cousins, the Monterey and knobcone, are known as fire pines, because they require the heat of fire to crack open their cones and release their seeds. Bishop pines are slow to propagate and are relatively rare in coastal California. (Another nice stand of Bishop pine is located in Montana de Oro State Park in San Luis Obispo County.)

Surest way to distinguish a Bishop pine from its look-alike, the Monterey pine, is by counting the needles: Monterey pines have three needles to a bunch, Bishop pines have two needles to a cluster.

From strategically placed benches, savor the fine bay views afforded by the Jepson Trail, which descends gently to Heart's Desire Beach.

Beauty by the bay: the rare Bishop pine

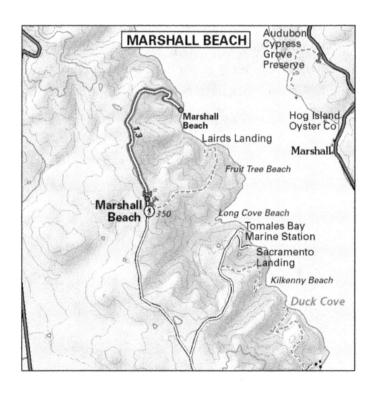

MARSHALL BEACH

Audubon Cypress Grove Preserve

Marshall Beach

Lairds Landing

Hog Island Oyster Co

Marshall

Fruit Tree Beach

1.3

Marshall Beach

.350

Long Cove Beach

Tomales Bay Marine Station

Sacramento Landing

Kilkenny Beach

Duck Cove

MARSHALL BEACH

MARSHALL BEACH TRAIL

From Duck Cove/Marshall Beach Road to Marshall Beach is 2.6 miles round trip with 300-foot elevation gain

Located off a road to nowhere on the bay side of the peninsula, Marshall is far from the easiest Point Reyes beach to reach. "This can't be the right road," is a frequently heard declaration from drivers.

Nearby Heart's Desire Beach with picnic facilities and drive-up access attracts almost all the visitors. Marshall Beach, off the beaten path, is a gem, a white sand fringed cove shaded by a stand of cypress.

(In addition to Marshall Beach Trail, a second dirt road departs the trailhead to Lairds Landing. Alas, several hundred feet of impassable rocky cliffs separate Marshall Beach from Lairds Trailhead and nix any possibility of a loop hike from Marshall Beach Trailhead.)

Local historians point out that Marshall Beach was named for local rancher Robert Marshall, who bought this spread in 1960, and not for the Marshall family that founded the town of the same name located across the bay.

Marshall will never be mistaken for a sunny Southern California-style beach, but the cove is protected by Inverness Ridge from wind and fog so sunning oneself on the beach here is not the laughable proposition it is elsewhere on the Point Reyes Peninsula. Joining hikers at Marshall Beach are kayakers, who paddle over from the hamlets across the bay or from the state park beaches to the south.

DIRECTIONS: From Highway 1 in Olema, head north 0.1 mile and turn left on Bear Valley Road. Proceed 2.2 miles to a junction with Sir Francis Drake Highway and head 5.5 miles west to a fork in the road. Bear right on Pierce Point Road and travel a mile to the Tomales Bay State Park entrance, continuing just past it to signed Marshall Beach Road. Turn right on this road (which soon turns to dirt) and drive 2.7 miles, following the "Park" signs through cow pastures to the signed trailhead.

THE HIKE: Pass through a stile and join the path (a wide ranch road) leading north. Marshall Beach Trail soon crests Inverness Ridge and offers good views over Tomales Bay. The road bends east toward the bay and, as if in a hurry to reach the beach, the road steepens as it descends toward the bay shore.

Considering all those hungry cows grazing above Marshall Beach, it's surprising to learn that a native coastal grassland continues to thrive on the rather bleak-looking ridges crossed by the trail. Pacific hairgrass, a hardy perennial beach grass, is a species that obviously rebounds well after grazing.

Wind-sculpted cypress extend a welcome to Marshall Beach. Note more cypress across the bay at Cypress Grove Preserve. And look up at the north end of Marshall Beach at porcelain-looking outcroppings of schist—among the oldest rocks of the peninsula.

You can walk south along crescent-shaped Marshall Beach until a prominent rock outcropping blocks further passage. And you can walk north to another secluded little beach.

Marshall Beach Trail: getting there is at least half the fun.

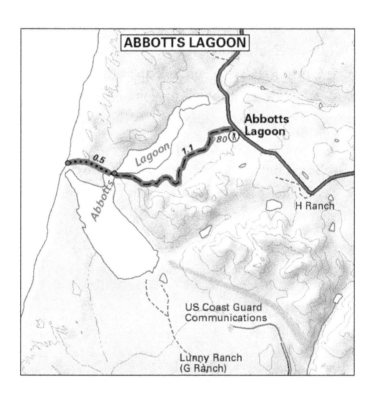

ABBOTTS LAGOON

Abbotts Lagoon

Abbotts

Lagoon

0.5

1.1

.80

H Ranch

US Coast Guard
Communications

Lunny Ranch
(G Ranch)

ABBOTTS LAGOON

ABBOTTS LAGOON TRAIL

From Abbotts Lagoon to Point Reyes Beach is 3.2 miles round trip

Something about Abbotts Lagoon personifies the word melancholy. Maybe it's the lagoon itself, a large, moor-like environment that compares to some of those I've visited by trail in Scotland. Then there are the lonely, wind-swept grasslands and the (perpetual, it seems) gray skies. It's the kind of place you photograph in black and white.

While a bit on the somber side, the lagoon and lands beyond are by no means dreary and depressing; in fact, the landscape encourages reflection—an inward journey to accompany a fine outer one. And spring is positively jubilant with abundant wildflowers, particularly California poppies, iris, and lots of lupine.

On a weekday excursion, your thoughts may very well be your only companion on this rather lightly visited trail, which leads 1.6 miles to Point Reyes Beach. A low ridge hides Abbotts Lagoon from the sight of passing motorists on Pierce Point Road; this positioning seems to discourage drop-in visitation of the kind that occurs elsewhere along the coast of the national seashore.

Gray-hued the lagoon may be, but it's anything but lifeless. Lots and lots of birds, both migratory and year-around residents congregate in an upper freshwater lagoon and a more brackish lower lagoon. Look for the western grebe and its pint-sized cousin, the pie-billed grebe, as well as lots of coots and terns.

If you can arrange a ride or car shuttle, a one-way hike (4.5 miles) from Abbotts Lagoon along the beach north to the Kehoe Beach Trailhead on Pierce Point Road is a great way to go.

Abbotts Lagoon seems to have a melancholy beauty all its own.

DIRECTIONS: From the hamlet of Olema, head north just 0.1 mile on Highway 1, then turn left on Bear Valley Road. Proceed 2.25 miles and fork left on Sir Francis Drake Highway. Drive 5.5 miles to Pierce Point Road, fork right and continue another 3.2 miles to the signed Abbotts Lagoon Trail and gravel parking lot on the left (west) side of the road.

THE HIKE: The wide, level trail leads across open fields. Gently rising, the trail offers better and better views of the lagoon. A well-located bench offers a fine place for quiet contemplation of water and wildlife.

The trail crests about the 0.8 mile-mark, then descends slightly to reach a bridge a mile from the trailhead. The footbridge bisects the upper and lower lagoons or as more lyrical naturalists refer to it—the wings of the lagoon.

From here an unmarked path edges around the base of the dunes between the wings of the lagoon to reach the ocean shores of Point Reyes Beach. Seals and sea lions have been known to snooze on this beach. Walk to your heart's content for miles, up-coast or down.

Northbound hikers can travel along the dune-lined beach about 2.8 miles to junction Kehoe Beach Trail, then hoof it another 0.6 mile to the trailhead on Pierce Point Road.

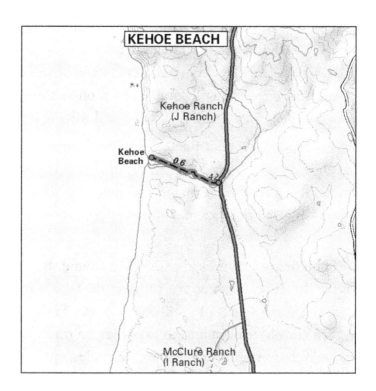

KEHOE BEACH

Kehoe Ranch
(J Ranch)

Kehoe
Beach

0.6

4.2

McClure Ranch
(I Ranch)

TheTrailmaster.com

KEHOE BEACH

KEHOE BEACH TRAIL

To Kehoe Beach is 1.2 miles round trip

More than a beeline to the beach, the trail crosses a watershed with many flowering plants, including yellow bush lupine and thickets of salmonberries with orange-reddish berries

Backed by dunes and dramatic bluffs, Kehoe Beach offers stellar hiking. Consider a one-way hike (4.5 miles) south to Abbotts Lagoon.

DIRECTIONS: Take Sir Francis Drake Highway to Pierce Point Road, and drive 5.5 miles to roadside pullouts for the Kehoe Beach Trailhead, located on the left (west) side of the road.

THE HIKE: The path descends the north side of Kehoe Marsh, passes a tiny lagoon, crosses the dunes at the 0.5-mile mark and descends to the beach. Walk the beach a short mile north or head south 2.8 miles to Abbotts Lagoon.

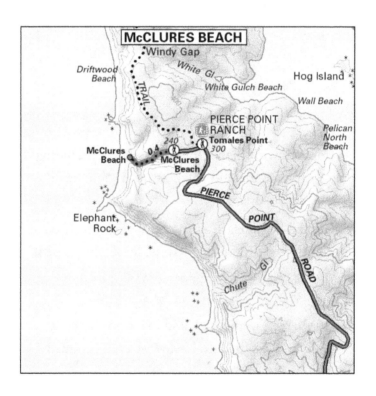

McClures Beach

McClures Beach Trail

To McClures Beach is 0.8 mile round trip

Way out on the northwestern shore of Point Reyes lies a beach that's positively theatrical: great granite cliffs, enormous rocks, huge waves. Exposed to the full fury of the Pacific, McClures Beach resounds with waves like rolling thunder that strike the rocks and sea stacks at land's end and toss great plumes of spray skyward.

DIRECTIONS: Take Sir Francis Drake Highway to meet Pierce Point Road and drive north 9 miles to the parking area for Pierce Point Ranch and Tomales Point Trailhead. Turn left on a winding access road and travel 0.3 mile to signed parking for McClures Beach.

THE HIKE: Hike the sandy, creekside trail to the center of 0.8 mile-long beach. Head south toward the sea stacks.

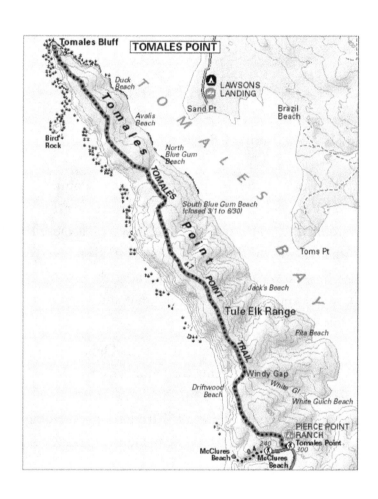

TOMALES POINT

Tomales Bluff

Duck
Beach

LAWSONS
LANDING

Sand Pt

Brazil
Beach

*Avalis
Beach*

T o m a l e s

Bird
Rock

*North
Blue Gum
Beach*

TOMALES

*South Blue Gum Beach
(closed 3/1 to 6/30)*

Toms Pt

P o i n t

POINT

Jack's Beach

Tule Elk Range

Pita Beach

TRAIL

Windy Gap

White Gl

*Driftwood
Beach*

White Gulch Beach

PIERCE POINT
RANCH

McClures
Beach

240

0.4

Tomales Point
300

McClures
Beach

TOMALES POINT

TOMALES POINT TRAIL

From Upper Pierce Ranch to Tomales Point is 9.4 miles round trip with 300-foot elevation gain

Tomales Point, solid granite carved by restless waves into bold cliffs, is quite the contrast to the softer slopes that comprise most of the California coast. Point Reyes has many distinguished "Points" but this is the most dramatic and a magnificent hike in all seasons: on a clear-winter day when the views are grand; in spring for the wildflowers; on those long summer days; in autumn when the tule elk are so active.

Tomales Point Trail, an old ranch road, wanders over the green hillocks that top the four-mile long finger of land thrusting northwesterly into the Pacific. The point, northernmost boundary of the national seashore, is seasonally sprinkled with yellow poppies, tidy tips and purple iris.

A tule elk herd roams the bluffs. The elk are usually found in two groups—a bull and his harem and in a congregation of bachelor bulls.

Solomon Pierce began a dairy in 1858, produced fine butter, and shipped it to San Francisco. Tomales Point Trail begins at Upper Pierce Ranch, where the Pierce family house, barn and outbuildings still stand.

DIRECTIONS: Drive north on Sir Francis Drake Boulevard past the town of Inverness. Shortly after Sir Francis turns west, bear right (north) on Pierce Point Road, and continue nine miles to its end at Upper Pierce Point Ranch.

THE HIKE: Begin at the signed trailhead near the old dairy buildings. The wide path passes near a windbreak of Monterey cypress and traverses grasslands

From Tomales Point Trail, hikers have a good chance of sighting the tule elk that roam the bluffs.

dotted with the ground-hugging blue lupine and showy, fragrant, yellow-flowered coastal bush lupine.

The trail climbs north across the coastal prairie and offers superb views of beach and surf. From the first hillock, observe McClures Beach and Elephant Rock.

A mile out, descend into aptly named Windy Gap and look down at also well named Driftwood Beach. The wide path climbs and descends at a moderate rate. Crest the ridge, drift over to its eastern side, and get views of Tomales Bay, as well as Hog Island and the village of Dillon Beach. At about the 2.2-mile mark, gain the trail's 540-foot high point.

Some 3.2 miles out, the old ranch road descends to the site of Lower Pierce Ranch, best identified by a pond and eucalyptus grove. The road becomes a trail and, about 0.4 mile past the ranch, arrives at a vista point that looks down on Bird Rock, occupied by cormorants and white pelicans.

About 3.9 miles from the trailhead, reach the end of the maintained trail. Continue on a somewhat sandy path, brightened in spring with California poppies and paintbrush. Elk trails and social paths made by fellow hikers cut across the main path and can lead the hiker to deadends.

The faint path climbs a last time at 4.3 miles, then descends the narrowing point to its very tip, a rocky perch about 30 feet above the Pacific. Stirring views of Bodega Head and Tomales Bay are the reward for reaching land's end.

Behold Bolinas Ridge: redwoods, sweeping grasslands, and an epic hike.

EVERY TRAIL TELLS A STORY.

V

HIGHWAY 1

HIKE ON.

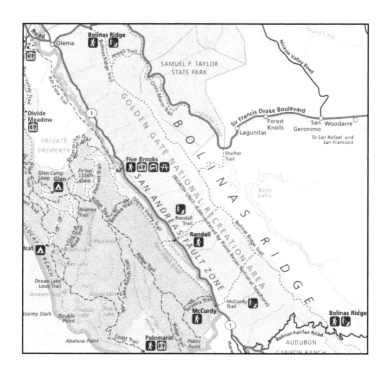

Bolinas Ridge

Bolinas Ridge Trail

From Olema to Bolinas-Fairfax Road is 11.2 miles one way with 1,200 foot elevation gain

Bolinas Ridge, a long finger of land bordered by Highway 1 and Pt. Reyes National Seashore on the west, is perhaps the Golden Gate National Recreation Area's most remote landscape. (BTW this wild northernmost part of GGNRA is administered by PRNS.) Ridge hikers are treated to dramatic vistas of Olema Valley to the west and the forested state parks—Mount Tamalpais and Samuel P. Taylor—to the east.

Long ago, Bolinas Ridge was heavily forested with redwood and Douglas fir; these trees, however, were logged and milled into lumber used to build San Francisco. The ridge these days is mostly grass-covered, dotted with coast live oak and remnant groves of Douglas fir and of second-growth redwoods.

From the ridge, the predominant view is of rolling hills, green in winter and spring and golden in summer and fall. The hills are bedecked with purple iris, gold California poppies and other wildflowers in spring.

The hills are dotted with cows, too. You may encounter cows along the trail and for sure you'll spot lots of cow patties. Watch your step.

True to its name, Bolinas Ridge Trail travels the ridge 11.2 miles from Olema to trail's end at Bolinas-Fairfax Road. Make this a long one-way day hike with a car shuttle or hike to one of the ridgetop's excellent viewpoints and turn around as time, and energy necessitates. The hike to Jewell Trail junction is 2.6 miles round trip; to Shafter Trail Junction is 10.2 miles round trip. I prefer hiking the entire trail because the ridge's redwoods are located along the southern sections of the trail.

The trail is a popular mountain bike route; however, Bolinas Ridge Road is a wide path and hiker-biker conflicts are minimal on this route. Dogs are allowed on this trail, and get quite a workout—along with their owners.

DIRECTIONS: From Highway 101 in San Rafael, exit on Sir Francis Drake Boulevard and drive west 17.5 miles to the trailhead on the left side of the road. Park carefully along the highway. The southern trailhead is located on Bolinas-Fairfax Road a few miles east of Highway 1.

THE HIKE: Join the ascending dirt road, which curves south through rolling grassland. Before long, views open up to the east of Olema Valley and behind you of Tomales Bay and Point Reyes Peninsula.

About 1.3 miles of hiking brings you to the top of the ridge and a junction with Jewell Trail, which drops east to Lagunitas Creek. Continue along the ridgetop a short distance farther for grand views west of forested Inverness Ridge and of Barnabe Peak in Samuel P. Taylor State Park.

Hike across open grassland with scattered small groves of coastal live oak, and note scattered reminders of cattle ranching—fences, chutes, corrals. After another mile along the ridge, hike in the company of Douglas fir growing on eastern slopes; the firs are more numerous and grow in thicker groves as you head south.

Four miles out, reach more open terrain, and then over the next mile, gain the ridgetop's high point, reach excellent vistas, and meet Shafter Trail. As noted, this junction is a good turnaround point if you're doing an out-and-back.

Onward to the redwoods and a meeting with Randall Trail in 1 mile, and with McCurdy Trail after hiking another 1.6 miles. Both trails drop 1,200 feet off Bolinas Ridge to reach Highway 1. Ah, the redwood forest, such a deeply shaded contrast to the open ridge. The tall trees are surrounded by a lush understory of ferns and clusters of Douglas iris.

From McCurdy Trail, it's 3.4 more miles to trail's end. Figure another pleasant mile or so through the redwoods then a transition to manzanita, ceanothus and a coastal chaparral community. The final 0.75 mile or so is back in the redwoods, a splendid way to end this wonderful adventure.

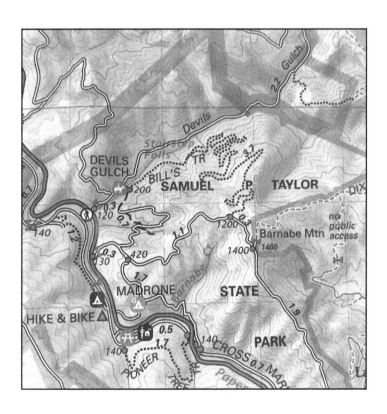

Samuel P. Taylor State Park

Bill's, Barnabe Trails

To Barnabe Peak via 6.5-mile loop with 1,400-foot elevation gain

From Barnabe Peak, you get a fire lookout's view: Pt. Reyes, National Seashore, Mt. Tamalpais, as well as lots more of central Marin County. The peak is the high point of Samuel P. Taylor State Park 2,700 acres of oak, tan oak and madrone woodlands, creekside redwoods, and open grassland.

Samuel P. Taylor came to California with the Gold Rush, making enough to capitalize construction of a paper mill on Lagunitas Creek, the first such mill west of the Mississippi. Taylor's Mill produced newsprint for the big San Francisco dailies, as well as better quality paper used in Sacramento for documents issued by the new state of California.

Eventually Taylor went into the resort business. During the 1870s and 1880s, Taylorville offered a new form of recreation: camping. Those preferring not to rough-it could stay in a three-story hotel. A narrow-gauge railroad came through Taylor's property, making it easy for city folk to reach his retreat, which became one of the most popular weekend getaways in Northern California.

Taylorville is long-gone, but the natural setting that made the resort so attractive to the city-weary of the last century remains equally attractive today.

Barnabe Peak honors explorer John C. Fremont's mule. Barnabe lived out his days as the Taylor family pet. The view from 1,466-foot Barnabe Peak provides an inspiring Marin County panorama. And the view is fairly unobstructed; Barnabe Peak, along with famed Mt. Tamalpais, are the only Marin County peaks with fire lookouts.

(It's not on this hike, but don't miss visiting the park's anything-but-satanic Devil's Gulch, heavenly shaded by oak, madrone and Douglas fir, with slopes brightened in spring with milkmaids, Indian paintbrush and buttercups.)

DIRECTIONS: From Highway 101, take the San Anselmon/Sir Francis Drake exit and travel 15 miles west Samuel P. Taylor State Park. Continue one mile past the main park entrance to a wide turnout on the left. Park here.

THE HIKE: Carefully cross Sir Francis Drake Boulevard and walk down the park service road. In 0.1 mile, angle right onto the footpath signed "Trail," then continue another 0.1 mile to a junction near the base of an enormous redwood. Note Barnabe Trail (our return route) leading right and cross the bridge over Devil's Gulch Creek

Begin a modest climb and enjoy the canyon's large trees: Douglas fir, big-leaf maple and even a small grove of eucalyptus. A mile out, a left-branching spur trail leads to Stairstep Falls, a 35-foot, three-tiered beauty.

Bill's Trail climbs on over a steep slope via a series of switchbacks. Two handsome bridges help you get across a steep ravine. Nearing the 4-mile mark, you finally emerge from the trees onto open grassland and soon thereafter meet Barnabe Trail (a fire road).

Turn left and ascend 0.3 mile to the top of Barnabe Peak and the fire lookout (private property). Take in the grand vistas of Tomales Bay and the greater Point Reyes peninsula, then return to the junction with Bill's Trail.

Continue a moderate to steep descent on Barnabe Trail over grassland that's seasonally dotted with such wildflowers as paintbrush, monkeyflower and California poppies. Except for one short ascent, it's all downhill hiking.

At about the 6-mile mark, pass a junction with the California Riding and Hiking Trail and soon thereafter spot a left-forking side trail that leads to the white picket fence enclosed gravesite of Samuel P. Taylor.

Barnabe Trail re-enters the woods and descends steeply to the first bridge and a junction with Bill's Trail. From here, retrace your steps to the trailhead.

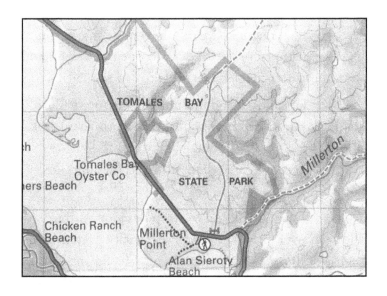

Alan Sieroty Beach & Millerton Point

Millerton Point Trail

From picnic ground to beach and Millerton Point is 1 mile loop

Hikers can gain an intriguing look at Tomales Bay via short paths above Alan Sieroty Beach, an isolated, 180-acre unit of Tomales Bay State Park. The beach was named for a longtime state legislator who was a very effective advocate for conservation causes.

The most obvious conservation cause promoted by the little-known park is aiding the endangered osprey. A short walk from the picnic area, the hiker encounters a specially constructed osprey nesting platform.

Some years ago, the ospreys insisted on nesting on PG&E's power poles and on occasion shorted out power to Inverness. The utility responded by erecting an osprey-friendly nesting site atop a nearby pole and gently enticing the birds to relocate. The birds soon moved—and nested—and today's visitor might just get a glimpse of the ospreys in their room with a view.

A large bird of prey often mistaken for an eagle, the osprey is a common sight along the shores of the Pt. Reyes Peninsula and Tomales Bay, but a few decades ago the birds were in big trouble. The osprey population declined precipitously with the use of agricultural pesticides (particularly DDT), but re-bounded after DDT was banned in 1972. Wildlife biologists follow the osprey's progress quite closely because the bird's acute sensitivity to pollution makes it an ideal "indicator species"—alerting scientists to degradation of the natural world.

Even if you don't spot an osprey, Millerton Point is worth a stop for a short walk or a picnic. Few travelers take the turnoff for Millerton Point (even though its marked) and you just might have the point, including its wetlands, eucalyptus trees and beach (not to mention a restroom) all to yourself, or share it with a few picnickers on the weekends.

Tomales Bay is THE place for oysters and the industry got started here a long time ago. In 1928, Tomales Bay Oyster Company made a first experimental planting at Millerton Point. Oyster aficionados like to buy them from TBOC (open Friday-Sunday), located only 0.75 mile north of Millerton Point and go picnic at the point, as well as at Heart's Desire Beach in the main part of Tomales Bay State Park.

DIRECTIONS: From the town of Point Reyes Station, take Highway 1 north 4.5 miles to the state park entrance on the left (west) side of the highway (15475 Highway 1)

THE HIKE: The loop trail (an old farm road) leads around Millerton Point, named for well-known early rancher James Millerton. Bird-watching is good from the trail, which extends along the perimeter of the point.

Spur trails lead to the beach. A few benches are perched at prime vista points. You can look across the bay at Heart's Desire Beach and other handsome sand strands, as well as the town of Inverness.

Millerton Point extends quite a ways into the bay and you're almost tempted to yell across the water to the people in "downtown" Inverness and let them know how peaceful it is here on the bay. Never mind. Likely they know that already, and are looking back at you.

Tomales Bay is THE place for oysters; Millerton Point was a location for an experimental planting in the 1920s.

Marconi Conference Center: Historic hotel offers bed, bath, and trails beyond.

MARCONI CONFERENCE CENTER STATE HISTORIC PARK

TOWER HILL, VISTA LOOP, MEADOW TRAILS

1 mile or so round trip

Marconi Conference Center State Historic Park, located a mile south of Marshall, offers a scenic meeting place while preserving a unique landmark in this history of global communication. The center features lodging, meals and a variety of meeting facilities.

The (non-conferencing) public is welcome to visit Marconi, and to walk its woodsy trails overlooking Tomales Bay. It's also now open for overnight stays.

In 1913, radio inventor Guglielmo Marconi picked a hillside above Tomales Bay for the site of his Pacific Coast receiving station in order to gather wireless messages from Asia, the Hawaiian Islands and ships steaming across the Pacific. The main building, known as the Marconi Hotel, was designed to resemble an Italian villa.

RCA owned the property in the 1920s, followed by ranchers and the Synanon Foundation, which purchased it in 1964 as a remote site for its rehabilitation work with substance abusers. The group's cult-like aspects came under fire and Synanon was accused of abusive treatment of the substance abusers it was supposedly helping.

Surely the group's most infamous act was to hide a rattlesnake in the mailbox of an opposing attorney; he was bitten, but recovered. A tiny local newspaper, *The Point Reyes Light*, covered—and uncovered—Synanon's activities and was awarded the Pulitzer Prize in 1979 for its exposé.

Lawsuits and public outrage forced Synanon to sell in 1981 and, after much complex negotiation, the property was acquired by the California State Parks Foundation, which turned it over to the state parks system for use as a conference center.

Ask for a map at the front desk, but know that the hiking here is strictly improvisational—a trail here, a walkway there, views wherever you find them.

Paths lead through oak woodland, across grasslands and up to vista points for grand view across Tomales Bay to Inverness Ridge in the national seashore. Watch for mule deer, plus lots of squirrels and rabbits.

DIRECTIONS: From the intersection of Highway 1 and Point Reyes-Petaluma Road in Point

Reyes Station, follow Highway 1 north 7 miles along the east side of Tomales Bay to the Marconi Conference Center on the right (east) side of the highway. Day-use visitors must park in the main parking lot.

THE HIKE: For a clockwise tour of the Marconi Center, join the walkway leading from the north side of the parking lot, follow Vista Loop Trail, and head up to the Antennae Site. Near the vista point, detour onto Lower Tower Hill Trail for a loop through a mixed woodland of coastal live oak and by laurel bay laurel, rich with an understory of elderberry and toyon.

Back at the top of Antennae Site, stay on the upper slopes with Tower Hill Trail, passing above Cypress Lodge and continuing to another vista point for views of Tomales Bay. The trail descends to the southern boundary of the conference grounds and meets Meadow Trail, which traverses a grassland community. Work your way back to the parking lot by walking past conference center buildings on well-named Conference Trail.

Set your sights on the long-billed curlew and many more birds at a trio of bird-watching preserves.

EVERY TRAIL TELLS A STORY.

VI

FOR THE BIRDS

HIKE ON.

Audubon Canyon Ranch

It's not unusual for coastal hikers to spot white egrets and great blue herons at the edges of California's bays, lagoons and estuaries. Audubon Canyon Ranch by Bolinas Bay offers an altogether different view of these big birds. Here the birds nest in the very tops of tall trees.

This tree-top colony, one of the major egret and heron rookeries on the California coast, can be observed by a viewpoint staffed by knowledgeable, sighting scope-equipped Audubon Society volunteers. To see and hear (parents and fledglings loudly squabbling) these big birds high up in the trees is to witness Nature at its most wonderful and most whimsical.

With 1,300 wooded acres, hiking trails, bay views, and fine wildflower displays in April and May, Audubon Canyon Ranch has much to offer the visitor. However, the Ranch's chief mission is to protect birds and serve as an outdoor laboratory for scientists. Thus, the preserve is open to the public only on weekends from mid-March through July.

BYOB (Bring Your Own Binoculars) to supplement the high-powered scopes set up at the observation point.

Although many visitors are content to walk to the overlook and check out the birds, hikers can enjoy some short hikes (1 to 3 mile loops) across grassland and chaparral and amidst redwood, oak and bay.

To make a bee-line for the birds, join Alice Kent Trail, which climbs moderately for 0.5 mile to the heronry overlook. After bird-watching at Henderson Overlook, you can return the way you came or by way of Rawlings Trail. This adds up to an easy one-mile family hike.

For a longer jaunt, head uphill through the woods on rather steep Rawlings Trail for 0.5 mile to a signed junction. Griffin Trail leads right but a better choice is to head left on Zumie's Loop (also called North Loop Trail). This path descends amidst ferns and redwoods and along a little creek. The trail climbs briefly to an open ridge and vistas of Bolinas Lagoon and the wide blue Pacific. The trail concludes with a mellow descent to ranch headquarters.

DIRECTIONS: From Highway 101 in San Francisco head north over the Golden Gate Bridge to the Highway 1/Stinson Beach exit. Follow Highway 1 about 12 miles to Stinson Beach, then continue another 3.5 miles north to the Audubon Canyon Ranch entrance on the right side of the highway.

Bolinas Lagoon

One of the few remaining unspoiled estuaries on the coast, Bolinas Lagoon is a vital stopover for multitudes of birds winging their way along the Pacific Flyway. The lagoon is located some 15 miles northwest of San Francisco and near the little town of Bolinas.

It's a good-sized lagoon, 1,100 acres, and in combination with Drakes Estero and Tomales Bay, offers an environment for resident and migratory birds unrivaled between San Francisco Bay and Humboldt Bay.

The western shore of Bolinas Lagoon is part of the Golden Gate National Recreation Area. Other portions of the lagoon are in Bolinas Lagoon Open Space Preserve administered by Marin County.

Breeding colonies of herons and egrets are among the most striking sights at the lagoon, where the bird count tallies some 245 species. Geese, ducks, and shorebirds winter at the lagoon.

Bolinas Lagoon isn't just for the birds. Harbor seals haul out to rest on the shores. Steelhead and coho salmon swim upstream to reach spawning grounds.

Hike Bob Stewart Trail (0.3 mile long) amidst alder and willow to the lagoon's north end. Not much hiking here compared to neighboring Audubon Canyon Ranch, where there are miles of trail. However Audubon Canyon Ranch is open only on the weekends from mid-March to July while Bolinas Lagoon is open all year around.

Bolinas Lagoon is a great place to canoe or kayak. Just make sure you know the tides or you and your watercraft could get stranded in mud in the middle of the lagoon. It's no fun getting stuck and forced wade in ultra slow motion through two-feet deep mud.

Bolinas Lagoon, which lies atop the San Andreas Fault, seems a good fit with the nearby town of Bolinas, a happy and relaxed place, and not one ruined by tourism. In fact locals have been known to tear down the sign for the town so tourists miss the turnoff and speed right by on Highway 1.

Bolinas Lagoon: home habitat and migration stop for many species of birds.

Point Reyes Bird
Observatory

"Location, location, location," is the key business advice often given anyone brave enough to open a restaurant. Remote bird sanctuaries, like convenient urban restaurants, also depend on a good location to attract their clientele.

Situated at the far southern end of the national seashore, some 30 miles west of the Golden Gate Bridge, Pt. Reyes Bird Observatory has an exceptionally good location at the intersection of several ecosystems (each of which attracts a variety of bird species).

Arroyo Hondo Creek bubbles through a fern-filled canyon that's rather rain forest-like with its water-loving plants and water-loving creatures such as newts and salamanders. Above the lush canyon bottom are three more environments—a coastal scrub community, a grassland and open ocean bluffs, all of which offer habitat and feeding opportunities for many resident and migratory birds.

The observatory welcomes the bird-loving public, but its chief mission is bird study; that is to say, using scientific inquiry to discover solutions to the many threats to birds, animals and their habitat. Palomarin Field Station's field biology program is regarded as one of the best in the U.S. Spring and summer months—breeding season—are particularly fine months for the public to visit the station and observe the research program in action.

For a short hike, join signed Fern Canyon Trail at the east side of the parking lot. The path stays on the blufftop for about 0.2 mile before it descends into a moist ravine watered by all-year Arroyo Hondo Creek. A bridge crosses the creek, which is lined with lady, sword, polypody (that's 'many feet" in Greek) and five-finger ferns. Many hikers poke around the lush canyon for a while then retrace their steps to the trailhead.

Otherwise, continue on the path as it ascends steps and switchbacks on the opposite side of Arroyo Hondo Creek, then meanders through a cluster of grand old buckeye trees to a meadow, believed to be the site of a Miwok Indian village.

DIRECTIONS: From Highway 1, some 5 miles north of Stinson Beach and about 9 miles south of Olema, turn west on the (usually unsigned) Bolinas-Fairfax Road, which you'll follow 1.3 miles along the edge of Bolinas Lagoon to Mesa Road. Turn right and drive 4 miles (the road de-evolves into gravel) to the Pt. Reyes Bird Observatory. Park in the lot.

"John McKinney tells the grand tale of the California coast like no one before him has done."

—Thomas Rigler, Executive Producer, *City Walk* and *California Coastal Trail* (PBS)

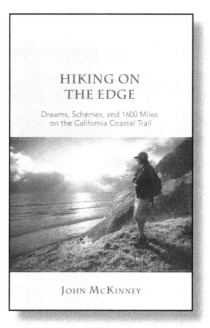

Hiking on the Edge: Dreams, Schemes, and 1600 Miles on the California Coastal Trail

A saga, a celebration, a comedy, a lament, this narrative ranks with the classics of California travel literature.

THETRAILMASTER.COM

- *Tips*
- *Tours*
- *Trails*
- *Tales*

JOHN MCKINNEY

John McKinney is an award-winning writer, public speaker, and author of 30 hiking-themed books: inspiring narratives, top-selling guides, books for children.

John is particularly passionate about sharing the stories of California trails. He is the only one to have visited—and written about—all 280 California State Parks. John tells the story of his epic hike along the entire California coast in the critically acclaimed *Hiking on the Edge: Dreams, Schemes, and 1600 Miles on the California Coastal Trail.*

For 18 years John, aka The Trailmaster, wrote a weekly hiking column for the Los Angeles Times, and has hiked and enthusiastically told the story of more than 10 thousand miles of trail across California and around the world. His "Every Trail Tells a Story" series of guides highlight the very best hikes in California.

The intrepid Eagle Scout has written more than a thousand stories and opinion pieces about hiking, parklands, and our relationship with nature.

A passionate advocate for hiking and our need to reconnect with nature, John is a frequent public speaker, and shares his tales on radio, on video, and online.

JOHN MCKINNEY:
"EVERY TRAIL TELLS A STORY."

HIKE ON.

TheTrailmaster.com